ON A RISING SWELL

UNIVERSITY PRESS OF FLORIDA

Florida A&M University, Tallahassee
Florida Atlantic University, Boca Raton
Florida Gulf Coast University, Ft. Myers
Florida International University, Miami
Florida State University, Tallahassee
New College of Florida, Sarasota
University of Central Florida, Orlando
University of Florida, Gainesville
University of North Florida, Jacksonville
University of South Florida, Tampa
University of West Florida, Pensacola

ON A
RISING SWELL

SURF STORIES FROM
FLORIDA'S SPACE COAST

Dan Reiter

UNIVERSITY PRESS OF FLORIDA

Gainesville/Tallahassee/Tampa/Boca Raton
Pensacola/Orlando/Miami/Jacksonville/Ft. Myers/Sarasota

Cover: Artwork by Jonas Claesson.

30 29 28 27 26 25   6 5 4 3 2 1

Library of Congress Cataloging-in-Publication Data
Names: Reiter, Dan R., 1977– author.
Title: On a rising swell : surf stories from Florida's space coast / by Dan Reiter.
Description: Gainesville : University Press of Florida, [2025] | Includes bibliographical references and index. | Summary: "In this high-speed glide through Florida surf culture, Dan Reiter chronicles stories of the sport in a region that has produced some of the world's finest surf champions, Pipe masters, and surfboard builders"—Provided by publisher.
Identifiers: LCCN 2024053252 (print) | LCCN 2024053253 (ebook) | ISBN 9780813080970 (paperback) | ISBN 9780813073750 (ebook)
Subjects: LCSH: Surfing—Florida—History—Anecdotes. | Surfing—Social aspects—Florida—Anecdotes. | Brevard County (Fla.)—History—Anecdotes. | Brevard County (Fla.)—Sports—Anecdotes. | Brevard County (Fla.)—Social life and customs—Anecdotes. | BISAC: SPORTS & RECREATION / Water Sports / Surfing | HISTORY / United States / State & Local / South (AL, AR, FL, GA, KY, LA, MS, NC, SC, TN, VA, WV)
Classification: LCC GV839.65.F5 R45 2025 (print) | LCC GV839.65.F5 (ebook) | DDC 797.3/2097592—dc23/eng/20241224
LC record available at https://lccn.loc.gov/2024053252
LC ebook record available at https://lccn.loc.gov/2024053253

The University Press of Florida is the scholarly publishing agency for the State University System of Florida, comprising Florida A&M University, Florida Atlantic University, Florida Gulf Coast University, Florida International University, Florida State University, New College of Florida, University of Central Florida, University of Florida, University of North Florida, University of South Florida, and University of West Florida.

University Press of Florida
2046 NE Waldo Road
Suite 2100
Gainesville, FL 32609
http://upress.ufl.edu

GPSR EU Authorized Representative: Mare Nostrum Group B.V., Mauritskade 21D, 1091 GC Amsterdam, The Netherlands, gpsr@mare-nostrum.co.uk

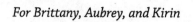

For Brittany, Aubrey, and Kirin

CONTENTS

"SURF LIT"

The psyche of a surfer is not a terribly complicated thing to wrap your mind around. First, imagine a toddler let loose in an open field. Now, install at one end of this field a bubble machine. Add a gentle breeze. The frolic that ensues, the wild yips and leaps of ecstasy, the breathless thrill every time a ball of liquid light bursts on the fingertips—there's the essence of it.

Increasingly, and in reputable circles, I've heard the phrase "surf literature" spoken out loud, and without a trace of irony. It seems to me a bit of a stretch to bank a genre on the theme of children chasing bubbles. Nonetheless, scribes have been wrestling waves and their riders onto the page for at least a few centuries now, with mixed results.

Eighteenth-century explorers and missionaries to the Pacific Islands—hypnotized by the sight of natives hauling their wooden planks out to sea and gliding back to shore on the incoming swell—were baffled by the idea that such a frivolous activity afforded these people places of eminence in their community. And yet, after observing one native's behavior, William Anderson, a surgeon on James Cook's 1777 expedition to Tahiti, tapped into this basic truth: "I could not help concluding that this man felt the most supreme pleasure while he was driven on, so fast and so smoothly, by the sea."

In 1907, Jack London visited Waikiki and paddled out with some locals, including George Freeth, who, along with Duke Kahanamoku, is largely credited for introducing the sport to the mainland. Here's London, waxing purple in "A Royal Sport: Surfing in Waikiki":

> And suddenly, out there where a big smoker lifts skyward, rising like a sea-god from out of the welter of spume and churning white, on the giddy, toppling, overhanging and downfalling, precarious crest appears the dark head of a man. Swiftly he rises through the rushing white . . . not buried and crushed and buffeted by those mighty mon-

sters, but standing above them all, calm and superb, poised on the giddy summit, his feet buried in the churning foam, the salt smoke rising to his knees, and all the rest of him in the free air and flashing sunlight, and he is flying through the air, flying forward, flying fast as the surge on which he stands. He is a Mercury—a brown Mercury. His heels are winged, and in them is the swiftness of the sea.

For the better part of three centuries, surf writing was a novelty act, far-flung reportage on an exotic pastime. But in 1957, a Hollywood screenwriter, Frederick Kohner, wrote a punchy, fictionalized account of his daughter's escapades with a crew of regulars at Malibu Point. The novel, *Gidget*, introduced surfing to a national audience and brought lingo like "shooting the curl" (racing across the vertical, pitching section of the wave), "pearl-diving" (when the nose of the surfboard goes under water), and "wipeout" into the lexicon. The 1959 movie adaptation, starring Sandra Dee, became a box-office sensation. Surf culture went viral. The flood of newbies into the lineups precipitated not only a surge of beach-themed movies but also reams of pulp surf fiction and how-to-surf books.

Hard-core surfers were not amused. Their literary riposte came in the form of *Surfer* magazine, a publication intended for real surfers, written by real surfers. Under the stewardship of filmmaker and publisher John Severson, *Surfer* went to print in 1960 and served as a template for generations of surf magazines to come—mesmerizing surf photographs set alongside essays, interviews, cartoons, tongue-in-cheek advertisements, board riding tips, and photojournalistic travelogues.

By the time Drew Kampion took the reins as *Surfer*'s editor in 1968, the counterculture had found its voice in its lustrous pages. Free-verse rambles like Kampion's "The Super Short, Uptight, V-Bottom, Tube Carving Plastic Machine" tuned into the frequency of the shortboard revolution,[1] drawing psychedelic, postmodernist lines in prose. "It is a rare surfer who surfs in the same style that he did last year," Kampion wrote. An apt credo for writers and riders alike.

In the '70s, Kevin Naughton and Craig Peterson, a couple of long-haired Huntington Beach teenagers, drove an old "wiped-out" Volkswagen Bug deep into Central America in search of uncharted, empty waves. Their travel dispatches for *Surfer* read like Hunter S. Thompson trips,

---

1 Shortboard revolution: the transition in the late '60s from heavy, longer boards to lighter, more maneuverable surfcraft.

only peppered with tiger sharks, El Salvadorian barroom debauches, and crystalline overhead barrels. Part picaresque, part chivalric romance, part road-trip epic, Naughton and Peterson's misadventures inspired a new generation of kids to drop out, pack their surfboards, and slide off to parts unknown. If surf literature can be judged on both merit and influence, these *Surfer* transmissions are about as close as you get to the pinnacle of the motif.

The best, and worst, surf writing has always played out in the mag-azines. Dig through any old-timer's rag collection, and you'll unearth a raft of titles—*Surfer, Transworld Surf, Surfing, Waverider, The Surfer's Journal, Longboard, Tracks, Rad, Aloha, Carve, Surf Girl, Eastern Surf, Southern Soul, White Horses* . . . Some were long-running institutions; others existed for only an issue or two. The surf mag was a niche format, its pool of talent limited to denizens of the intertidal zone (hardly a well-read demographic). Leaf through too many back issues and you begin to feel supersaturated. How many ways can you depict "a radical hack off the lip" or, as London wrote in *Ladies' Home Journal,* "the marching billows, the smoking crests, the white battalions of the infinite army of the sea"? Nevertheless, these glossies—which have gone nearly extinct in the internet era—were a place where surfers could swing their pens freely, where captions read like haikus, interviews like conversations with the Buddha, and where fustian poems were natural extensions of jaw-dropping photos of 20-foot Sunset Beach bombs.

While autobiographies of famous surfers like Kelly Slater and Gerry Lopez make for fascinating reading to the initiated—and outliers like Allan Weisbecker's drug-addled *In Search of Captain Zero* (2001) and David Rensin's biography of Miki Dora, *All for a Few Perfect Waves* (2009), are wildly entertaining romps through the underbelly of the surfer's path—precious few works of surf memoir have played to a broader audi-ence. The inside angles are too esoteric. Either you get it or you don't. You're in or you're out.

As to fiction, the repertory is thinner still. A standout that comes to mind is Kem Nunn's 1984 surf-noir *Tapping the Source,* but even I would be hard-pressed to name my top five surf novels.

One unicorn of a surf story, William Finnegan's "Playing Doc's Games," appeared in the *New Yorker* in 1992. It was a long-form journalistic fea-ture that summoned the wind-whipped peaks of San Francisco and the die-hard commitment of the Ocean Beach surfer. Finnegan wrote in a nuanced, journalistic style that proved palatable to café culture. Here, he evokes the pride of punching through the inside section, where ferocious cold-water waves explode on the shallow sandbar and deny the unfit: "All had passed the snarling mastiff of the inside bar—the price of admission to this green-gold world of glassy low-tide peaks." Not bad, as surf lit goes. Finnegan's surf-centric memoir, *Barbarian Days,* won the Pulitzer Prize in 2015, sending out ripples of credibility among the intelligentsia and cementing his position as Grand Vizier of the Dubious Canon.

Perhaps the internet will lay waste to all literary genres, in the end. Just as Finnegan's opus was making the rounds, the prestige surf magazines were rasping out their last breaths. *Surfing* shut down in 2017 after more than fifty years in print; *Surfer* took its last drop in 2020, at the age of sixty. Only stray survivors remain in print today: *Carve* in the United Kingdom; *Surfing Life, Tracks,* and *Surfing World* in Australia; *The Surfer's Journal* in the United States. With unlimited quantities of surf content available at a finger's touch to anyone with a cell phone, the surf magazines, out of necessity, are doubling down on quality. *The Surfer's Journal* fields master wordsmiths like Jamie Brisick and Scott Hulet, and world-class photographers like Grant Ellis and Todd Glaser. The dying gasp of print culture has become a sumptuous, atavistic reduction, and the remnants are regularly producing some of the highest-grade stuff in the history of the medium.

Boiled down to its essence, the sensual elements of surfing will always be rich: the coconut smell of surf wax, a wetsuit drip-drying in the sun, coffee vapor mingling with salt mist, the gleam and crackle of an outside set on a windless morning. One of the best arguments for the legitimacy of surf literature is that surfing has its own idiosyncratic language, a patois, and that it fully inhabits its own universe.

The Web is not completely barren territory, either. Matt Warshaw, a former editor of *Surfer,* has compiled an online encyclopedia of surf history and vernacular with comprehensive entries ranging from "A-frame" (peak-shaped wave, generally short, hollow, and powerful; ridable in either direction—left or right) to "Zamba, Frieda" (affable but resolute goofyfoot[2] pro surfer from Flagler Beach, Florida; four-time world champion). And blogs and industry-backed websites have helped fill the void created by the death of the surf magazine, providing a forum for surf writers to unleash their howls in real time.

---

2   Goofyfoot: a term used to describe a surfer who rides with their right foot forward and their left foot on the tail of the board. The opposite stance is called "regularfoot."

It is typical of surfers, particularly Florida surfers, to reminisce on sessions gone by as if they were unfathomable, irreproducible events. To hear someone speak of the '91 Halloween Swell, for example, is to submit to the familiar cadences of Bible verse or mythology. Not surprisingly, the dwindling cadre of surf journalists are experiencing similar pangs of nostalgia for the era of the surf magazine. In recent years, the publishing presses have been spooling out collections by grizzled magazine veterans who staked their lives reporting for the tribe. The cream of surf literature can be found in some of these volumes, in the descriptions of waves of consequence or the textures of mysterious offshore barrels and clandestine reefs. This year alone, Matt George, Steve Pezman, and Ralph Sneeden published collections of surf-themed essays. Scott Hulet, the longtime editor of *The Surfer's Journal,* and one of my favorite scribblers of surf lit, is set to release a hardbound omnibus this year. And good old Naughton and Peterson, now in their late sixties, are putting out a retrospective of their travels for *Surfer* as a trio of coffee-table books.

What you are about to read is not one of those books. There are no surf photographs, none in high-gloss color, anyway. It is not the reportage of a veteran surf journalist, nor the exploits of a professional surfer. Neither is it a dedicated atlas of surf history, a how-to manual, or a memoir (it imitates the personal narrative in the next chapter, but the reader will find the form short-lived). This book is, rather, a collection of surf-adjacent vignettes, hasty dispatches scrawled over chai lattes by a writer of short fiction—often at the Café Surfinista in Cocoa Beach, in the postcoital thrall after a surf session. Some of these pieces originally ran in a monthly Cocoa Beach paper called the *Beachside Resident.* Others were published by *Eastern Surf Magazine, Surfer,* and *The Surfer's Journal.* They are inside jokes, abbreviated histories and revelations, fragments of interviews, free-floating sketches braided together only by the tenuous thread that is surfing, and specifically surfing in this subtropical zone between Cape Canaveral and Sebastian Inlet, Florida. Together, they form a paean to the Space Coast—this insignificant, dribbly waved stretch of sand that has somehow spawned an impossible number of world surfing champions, Pipe masters, and iconic surfboard builders—where the coconut palms occasionally freeze in winter, and where it is not uncommon to witness a rocket launch from the comfort of your surfboard.

Florida's East Coast.

Illustration by Thibaud Jacquier-Bret.

Firsts

~~~~~~

Live beachside long enough and you'll come to appreciate how an environment that can pulverize iron and turn stainless steel to rust will ultimately wreak similar physiological changes on the human body. Lashed by sun and salt, the supplest skin weathers to a deep-creased, mottled rind of leather. The brilliant white of the eye's sclera blooms with red pterygiums—a condition known as "surfer's eye." Or surfer's ear develops: the growth of a hard, bony exostosis in the inner ear.[1]

Coastal air isn't altogether malevolent, though. Psychologist and ion particle researcher Michael Terman, PhD, theorizes that exposure to the sea breeze can actually make a person happier. "The action of the pounding surf creates negative air ions," Terman explains, "just as immediately after spring thunderstorms, people report lightened moods."

White noise and atomized wave-spray assuredly alter your perspective. I'm convinced they are capable of modifying your genetic blueprint as well. In any case, twenty years of brine, of salt marinade, of inhaling the sea's musk, have permanently transformed me.

---

1   Surfer's ear was endemic in many Indigenous watermen tribes, including the Ais (ah-ees) of Central Florida, some of whom spent eight hours a day diving for oysters and lion's paw scallops.

FIRST WAVE—OCEAN BEACH, SAN FRANCISCO

I'm a Canadian, Montreal born. When I was three years old, my family immigrated to South Florida, where I grew up on the rain-darkened fringe of the Everglades swamps, in a town called Plantation, 20 miles and three freeways away from any coastline. I never surfed as a child. My earliest memories of the beach come from family visits to my Yiddish grandparents' condominium in Hallandale Beach. They were Holocaust survivors, and neurotically overprotective of me and my two sisters, so they kept us immured on the pool deck, tucked safely under the blue-striped umbrellas and the watchful eyes of old Jews playing shuffleboard to Engelbert Humperdinck tunes. A white stucco wall with peek-holes barricaded us from the open sea. On the rare occasion that we were allowed to pass through the gates and step into the hot, waveless Atlantic, we were instructed not to wade out past our knees. My Bubbe had crossed that same Atlantic Ocean in the bowels of a refugee boat—pregnant, seasick, and near death the whole time. She couldn't swim, and her aquatic terrors transmitted subconsciously, supplying me with years of recurring nightmares in which I was ripped from the sand by a vicious undertow and drowned in the shorebreak.

I didn't catch my first wave until I was twenty-two. I'd recently graduated college with a degree in English and was more or less drifting . . . no career ambitions, no connections. Reluctant to start a life as a responsible adult, I hitched a ride out west with some actors and film students I'd met in New York City. High on romantic visions of the Beats and the Merry Pranksters, we swept across the country like windblown dandelions, fluttering wildly toward San Francisco. When we landed in Haight-Ashbury, we found those golden sidewalks had become a blighted pincushion of heroin addicts and pit bulls, and all the rainbows had been trampled to dust. Kerouac was dead, Kesey was on his way out. Worse still, the tonier parts of the city had been whitewashed by the tech boom, scraped bare of truth by trust fund kids from Sausalito.

I bluffed my way into a bartending job in the Marina district and moved into what you might call a sunroom—or a walk-in closet—in a three-bedroom apartment off the Panhandle. My roommates were three friends from high school, each of whom had a full-time job and an actual bedroom. A few nights a week I poured drinks. The rest of the time I read yellowed Russian novels in coffee shops, dropped acid, and wandered the Golden Gate Park or the foggy Potrero. I was some kind of fool.

My metamorphosis began one afternoon in late August, when my roommate, Aaron, suggested I go out to Ocean Beach and surf with him. I'd never surfed before, never read a surf magazine, or even watched a surf video. Aaron drove me to the end of Fulton Street, to Wise's Surf Shop, where we rented 40-pound monstrosities, yellow-and-blue water-logged soft-top longboards.

Aaron had his own wetsuit, but I would need to rent one. Renting a wetsuit is a foul, repulsive thing to do for manifold reasons, not least being the tradition of surfers relieving themselves inside them.

"What do you wear under it?" I asked the dude at the shop.

"Usually nothing," he replied.

One cannot understate the contortions and calisthenics required of a novice trying to fit into a rented 4/3 wetsuit (a cold-water suit: 4-millimeter-thick neoprene in the torso and 3 millimeters in the arms and legs). I twisted, grunted, nearly dislodged my shoulder, hopped on one leg, then the other, and fought the unwieldy, bacteria-infested outfit for a good five minutes before stiffly emerging from the changing room, only to be informed that I had put it on backward.

The salesman helped us strap the longboards onto the roof of Aaron's car and wished us luck. We rolled out to the nearest surf spot, a place called Seal Rocks, where white-peaked boulders plastered with bird shit rose like little snowy mountains from the sea. Aaron gave me the five-minute surfing primer in the parking lot. Strap the leash to your ankle. Lie down on your stomach on the board. "When the wave comes, you paddle like this," he demonstrated. "Paddle, paddle, then pop up! Feet sideways, on the center stringer."

I practiced pouncing onto the deck a couple times, rubber fins squealing on the asphalt. "Okay," I said. "I'm ready." We shuffled over the concrete barrens, balancing our massive crafts atop our heads.

Aaron had surfed before, but like me, he was a kook, a novice, a VAL.[2] Experienced surfers will typically study the ocean for ten to twenty minutes before attempting to paddle out at a new spot, timing the period of calm between sets, and watching for rip currents and channels that might allow them an easier passage through the breakwaters. We did no such thing. The fact that the waves were overhead and pumping that day, and that we were attacking one of the heavier surf spots in California, couldn't have been more beside the point. We sallied forth like Cirque du Soleil clowns, backpedaling a moment in the churn of the shallows, then jumping onto our boards, windmilling our arms like maniacs and stroking straight into the washing machine.

Kooks are, at best, oblivious idiots; at worst, they can be menaces to the lineup.[3] That day, we stood no real chance of making it to the outside and so presented no danger to anyone but ourselves. When the first curtain of whitewater hit us, the noses of both our boards shot up, and we flipped backward in unison. The impact of the cold water was shocking. I felt like an unsuspecting wide receiver slammed down by a linebacker. The wave threw me from my board, smashed me against the sand at the bottom, held me underwater, and tried to wrench my leg from my hip socket by the leash. My mouth opened of its own accord, and I took in a full gulp of the foul, freezing water. It gushed up my nose and shot into my brainpan. I somersaulted and struck sand again. My lungs began to burn, and I felt that same suffocating panic from my childhood nightmares. For a moment, my body seemed to be rising toward the surface . . . I perceived a greenish glow that I hoped might be the sky, but then the horror returned—another onslaught, a blackout—and I was pitched a second time to the ocean floor. I might have died then and there, but the sea mercifully released me, gasping and retching in waist-deep water.

Out there, in the blue and placid distance, the surfers bobbed like meditative seals. A calmness had flattened the waters, and the surf zone seemed clear enough now for me to paddle out and join them. Once again, I leaped on my board and scrambled for the deep water. But before I could make any headway, more black and menacing hills swelled on the horizon. The surfers went scratching down the wave faces, tracing

---

2 VAL (Vulnerable Adult Learner): a surf-insider euphemism for a clueless late-comer to the sport.

3 Lineup: the area just beyond the breaking waves where surfers sit and wait for the sets.

bright-white slashes out there, impossibly far out to sea. I could only see them at intervals between the rises in the water. Then the spindrift flared up, the waves combusted, and more white chaos rampaged toward me. Time and again, I was tossed, dashed, rolled, denied at the rabid jaws of the "snarling mastiff." When I could handle no more, I sat atop my board, wobbling, panting, my arms heavy as clay, ropes of crazed white-water sloshing everywhere. Which way was shore?

"Ah, there you are!" I cried, spotting Aaron in a similar position. "Is the water supposed to leak into your wetsuit like this?"

I'll never forget his face in that moment: a smile of surrender, of commiseration, the type of smile you might see as the airplane is going down. He pointed out to sea, and there it was—the big one, bearing down on us like an avalanche. "Go!" he shouted.

Aaron lay down on his belly and clutched the sides of his soft-top. I did the same. The air warped and detonated behind me. I felt myself plunging. I gripped my board. My chin smacked the deck. The wave bounced and bullied me toward shore. After the initial crush, I hopped to my feet, as I had been trained. And for two or three transcendent seconds, I was flying. Like a golden god. Like Queen Lili'uokalani herself.

Then I pearl-dived, and once again rag-dolled into the maelstrom.

FIRST GLIMPSE OF THE DHARMA—
SUNSET POINT, LOS ANGELES

It was the summer of 2001, and one of the film students I'd ridden out west with—a stout, long-haired, basso profundo character by the name of Todd Smolar, who would later go on to man the velvet ropes at Manhattan's famed Beatrice Inn—had set up a makeshift commune in a Topanga Canyon ranch house under the pretense of a dog-sitting job for Ken Kaufman, the screenwriter of *Space Cowboys*. Todd invited me to stay the summer with him, and I abandoned my bartending job and sunroom in San Francisco to hole up in Topanga with a rotating crew of musicians and lunatics.

We slept anywhere—on futons, on the floor, in the front yard—played guitar noon through night, and were generally lax about things like doing the dishes or closing the doors. I was twenty-three years old, young and wild and unstrapped, and I'd finally found the California I'd been looking for, a Bohemia of beads, booze, butterflies, and bonfires. This was before the Twin Towers fell, before the center ceased to hold, before it became obvious to everyone that the empire was in the process of collapsing. None of us had social media. No one was keeping score. We could drink and smoke and make love and make mistakes and none of it would matter so long as we cleaned it all up in the end.

One of the regulars at the Topanga complex was a blue-eyed leading-man type by the name of Philip Salick, who was renting a clapboard shack up in the live oaks with his girlfriend. I would find out years later that Philip's father, Rich Salick, and his uncle (also named Phil) were legendary watermen in Florida—identical twins—who had shaped Kelly Slater's first surfboard. Young Philip had been a semi-pro surfer himself on the East Coast contest circuit as a teenager. He also happened to be a generous, exceedingly patient surf instructor to Todd and me.

Every day that summer, after we'd brewed our noontime coffee and cooked up some toast and scrambled eggs, Philip would saunter down the pine-needle path, help us load the boards, and ride with us down the winding canyon road to the beach.

Sunset Point is a kook-friendly spot at the end of Sunset Boulevard in LA, with easy access to the lineup if you climb down the rocks. One windless day, with the water glazed to brushed glass, and the sets a manageable 3–4 feet, we followed Philip into the cool water of the cove, where he showed us how to use the rocks as a sight line to position ourselves. Unlike a beach break, a point has a specific takeoff zone. The waves peel reliably, consistently. We sat to the right of the main peak, on the shoulder of the wave, and observed the other surfers from behind. They swung to the right, and their heads sailed along for a quarter mile or more, always tracking the same line.

"I'm going to catch one," Philip said, stroking over to the peak. "When you see me on it, just go. I'll ride behind you."

A wave came, on cue, as waves tend to come for the best surfers. With a graceful springing motion, Philip was up and riding. I followed his instructions and was amazed at how smooth my entry was. Instead of dropping straight down the face of the wave, I was able to angle my board, pop to my feet, and trace a high line toward the shoulder.

Riding a wave straight in to shore—standing on your feet and stuttering at the leading edge of the lather—is, technically, surfing, but hitching yourself to the glassy part of a wave, slicing the prismatic wall, is another realm completely. Every surfer remembers their first time going down the line. For me, it happened that day at Sunset Point. A moment of disbelief, a lightness, a softening of time and reality. You might compare it to first love. It is the dharma, the essence, the all-knowing mandala. Surfers call it "stoke."

I would have been content to stay forever young and barefoot in Topanga Canyon. But Kaufman, the screenwriter, would be home from Europe soon, and no one wanted to be around when his wife found out which dresses the girls had "borrowed" from the master bedroom closet. It was August or so, and the last of the party, maybe fifteen of us, had gathered in the family room. We were watching a surf movie, *Longer*, starring Joel Tudor, when I got the call from my grandfather.

"What are you doing in California?" he asked me. He ignored my feeble attempt at an answer. "It's *meshuggeneh!* You need to get a job!"

What my grandfather wanted to know was if I would come back to Florida. His partner needed help on a construction job in Tampa. It was a chance to learn the construction business before he was too old to teach me. He was pushing ninety but still driving across Alligator Alley, three hours in the car from Hallandale to Tampa, at least once a month, still climbing ladders, still inspecting roof shingles. "Just come for one year," he told me. "It would be a big help."

"The worst part about it is that I'm not going to be able to surf," I lamented to Philip later that night. "It's always flat in Florida."

Philip raised an eyebrow. "It might be flat in South Florida," he said. "The Bahamas block the swells. But you should check out Cocoa Beach. You'd be surprised . . . they actually have surf there."

FIRST SURFBOARD—COCOA BEACH, FLORIDA

I ended up moving to Tampa, and every weekend I took the two-hour drive east, following the Ron Jon billboards across I-4 and the Beeline Expressway, over two bridges, and onto the barrier island. I'd rent a board and take it to the place I assumed to have the best waves (since it was the most crowded spot in town): the Cocoa Beach Pier.

It's safe to say those first days in Cocoa Beach—back when everything quivered with newness, when I was still a kook, a weekend warrior—I believed all the secrets of life could be read in that pier, that sibylline jumble of teetering lumber dipping its barnacled legs in the silty waters. Especially of a midmorning, when the parade of characters would filter across the sands—the pious, the profane, the workers, the tourists, the itinerants—come to loll and skim and toss their lines, to smear themselves and sunbathe and clomp the planks and linger under the thatched roof of the Rikki Tikki Tavern and gape at the water dancers.

I still retain a vivid picture of my first session at the pier. The wind was onshore, the waves negligible—2–3-foot slop—but the surfers were finding improbable pockets of speed and noseriding with more skill and flair than anyone I'd seen in California. The dunes looked like white snowdrifts, and I remember the seething heat of the sand and the feeling of some subterranean energy thrumming beneath my feet.

The girl at the rental shop had told me the secret to paddling out at the pier: stick close to the pilings, and the current will pull you out unscathed. It worked, and I floated for a time on the outside, sunning myself (wetsuits are rarely necessary in Cocoa Beach, maybe only one or two months out of the year), marveling at the bend of the cape and the darkling monoliths on the northern horizon. The peaks were jumbled and wind-wrecked, yet a flow and harmony abided in the lineup. Eventually, a wave swung my way, and I caught a miraculous left that carried me farther than should have been possible.

I surfed that day until I couldn't lift my arms anymore. I lay down on the beach and napped in the sun. Then I surfed some more. Everything seemed to validate the refrain that had been playing in my head since that first day at Sunset Point: all I wanted to do with my life was surf.

A few months later, tired of the predawn trek from Tampa every Saturday morning, I rented a one-bedroom sand-catcher on Fifth Street South in Cocoa Beach. The apartment had a leaky AC window unit and a grievous palmetto bug problem. It wasn't modern luxury—none of the appliances worked—but it was directly across the street from the beach access, and would serve as a sort of chrysalis for me, a preparatory stage for my life to come. I dropped a mattress on the floor; it was good enough.

When you wake up every morning to the sound of the waves, the world takes on a sheen like hammered gold. Cocoa Beach was in full bloom that fall: pink and white oleander, strutting peacocks, poinciana trees tangled in sunlight, the syrupy smell of jasmine vines, and the occasional 80-foot-tall cabbage palm swaying gently on high. All set to the rhythmic shush of the sea.

I was beginning to suspect that Ron Jon was not a fully "authentic" surf shop, so when the time came to buy my first surfboard, I went down to a shop called the Longboard House, in Indialantic. They carried beautiful, artisanal pieces—Hap Jacobs, Takayamas, McTavishes—but these were too expensive, and I asked for something more affordable. The salesman tagged me as an easy mark and persuaded me into purchasing a 9'0" epoxy Walden. Looking back, there's a sad irony in my buying a pop-out surfboard[4] when some of the most talented shapers on the planet operated shops right there in Cocoa Beach. But I hadn't grown a brain yet. The legendary surf history of this town, the taproot of East Coast waterman culture . . . that would all come later. For now, I was a bewildered fish in shallow waters.

In those days, the south Cocoa Beach streets were still manufacturing A-frame waves that peeled from the outer bar to the beach, through high tide or low (the sandbars hadn't yet been wrecked by hurricanes, storm

---

4   Pop-out surfboard: a machine-shaped, assembly-line glassed board usually made in China, or anywhere loose child labor laws and lack of environmental regulations allow for cheaper, quicker production than local, handmade craftsman pieces.

surges, or dredge hoppers). Some of the midbreak swims were rough. Many days I got pounded, stunned, beaten, but I kept paddling out, day after day, and I kept learning.

I'd gained a rudimentary understanding of the rules of surf etiquette, about deferring to the surfer closest to the peak and not "dropping in" (taking off on the wave someone is already riding), but awareness does not always guarantee competence. One day, I drifted closer than I should have to a pack of stylish longboarders. Unmindful of a white-bearded, leashless fellow who had caught one of the set waves and was already up and flying, I took off on his wave, saw him too late, nearly decapitated him as I kicked my epoxy banana board in the air, and ended up floating in the whitewater next to him. I was mortified. I paddled over to apologize.

"For what?" the old salt said.

"For ruining your wave."

He looked at me incredulously, recovered his board, knee-paddled out to sea, and shouted one of the most charitable phrases I've ever heard in the ocean: "Forget it, there's thousands of waves!"

If the birth of wisdom is admitting you know nothing, the same can be said of learning to surf. First, you must recognize your own absurdity. Only then can you embark upon on the path to enlightenment.

How to Be a Kook

I wrote this satirical piece for the *Beachside Resident* in 2011, back when
I was still learning how to distinguish competence from stupidity.
Neophytes might read it as a catalogue of behaviors to *avoid* when
learning to surf.

Kook \kük\ (n): **1** one whose ideas or actions are eccentric, fantastic, or ill-advised. **2** in surfing parlance, a beginner.

Step 1. Head to Your Nearest Surf-Megaplex

Need directions? Easy—just drive east from Orlando on the Beachline Expressway and follow the billboards. If your surf-megaplex has advertisements on the highway, it's a sure bet it will carry the equipment you need. Weekends are your best chance to find primo boards . . . and, lucky for you, the gnarliest waves!

Step 2. Rent Your Board

Top-quality surfboards are usually kept in the back for expert surfers, so you'll need to talk savvy. A good opening line might be, "Buoys are rocking, brah, I guess I'll need a blue beast." If the salesman asks for clarification, lean in conspiratorially and say, "I'll take the biggest board in your quiver, dude. And the more fins the better." This should convince him. He will lead you to his secret stash.

Step 3. Select Your Wetsuit

Rubber stretches over time, so you'll want an older wetsuit for better maneuverability. Request one size larger than the salesman suggests. If he asks you to try it on, tell him, "No time, dude, I gotta catch me some bitchin' barrels before the wind switches offshore!"

Party wave?

Illustration © John Klossner. www.jklossner.com.

Step 4. Locate Your Secret Surf Spot

No worries, brah! Below is a list of the most top-secret, most killer, locals-only surf beaches within driving distance from Orlando:

Ponce Inlet
Canaveral Pier
Coconuts on the Beach
2nd Light
RC's
Indialantic Boardwalk
Sebastian Inlet
Spanish House

Sebastian Inlet is by far the most consistent wave, and well worth the extra drive time (hey, why not throw down a six-pack on the way home?), but any of these spots will do in a pinch. When in doubt, remember: the bigger the crowd, the better the waves!

Step 5. Don Your Gear

More than likely your wetsuit will have a zipper in the front. Always try it on this way first. If you are still unsure, ask a fellow surfer how it looks. You will need his assistance anyway. Never try to zip up a wetsuit by yourself. (Wetsuit pro tip: Always urinate in your wetsuit the moment you zip it up. This "dry-pee technique" will help you retain body heat for your epic session.) Once you are zipped up and peed out, lay your surfboard flat on the asphalt and stand on top of the deck. If you're feeling adventurous, walk to the nose and "hang ten." This is sure to impress any onlookers.

Now that you're comfortable with your surfboard, strap on your leash. (The leash goes on the leg opposite from your carrying arm. If you decide to carry the board over your head, the leash goes on your left foot. If it's extra windy, switch it to your right.)

Step 6. Paddle Out

A true kook won't break stride from the parking lot to the ocean. If you see other surfers sitting on the crossover and watching the waves, don't engage them. They're probably posers, anyway. Give them the stink eye. Don't worry if the waves look daunting—they always look bigger from the beach. Never hesitate—*always* go for it! Expert tip: The easiest paddle-out is where the crowd is thickest; this is probably where the channel is. When the waves are macking, you might have a tough time paddling all the way to the outside. Be persistent. Whenever a set wave or another surfer comes toward you, ditch your board, dive as deep as you can, wait it out, then reel in your leash, cough out the saltwater, climb back on, and keep paddling. Eventually there will be a lull in the sets. If not, just set up shop on the inside, as close as you can to the main pack.

Step 7. Cowabunga!

Now that you're out in the lineup, show everyone how radical you are by catching the first wave that comes your way. (You'll know a wave is good if one of the local surfers is paddling for it.) To catch a wave, lie down on your stomach and stroke as fast as you can toward shore; when you feel the wave begin to take you, pop up on one knee, then two knees, then one foot, then both feet.

Important: stance is everything. Study pictures of big wave chargers at Mavericks or Waimea, and you'll notice the feet set wide apart, the knees bent 90 degrees. This pose, known as the "stinkbug," is the most balanced position and will distinguish you as a master-class surfer.

Step 8. Claim It

After a sick ride, or after a sick takeoff followed by a sick wipeout, the proper etiquette is to "claim" your wave by whooping, pumping your fists over your head, and giving the double-middle-finger salute while shouting obscenities to anyone within earshot. Other surfers who were paddling for your wave might even show their respect by echoing your sentiments.

Step 9. Carry It with You

Don't leave your attitude out in the water. The spirit of kookdom should flow through your everyday life, in the way you lean up against your car while texting a honey ("tore it up @ da pier 2day"), in the careful sideways tilt of your hat, in the Salt Life and Volcom stickers on your car, in the sparkle of your cubic zirconia earrings, in the way you flick your Parliament Lights out your window, or how you casually toss empty cans of Natty Light on the dunes before retiring to the strip club after a vigorous twenty-minute session.

Most of all, keep at it. It can take months to find the ideal facial expression that shows just how badass you are while sitting on your board. And it could be years before you perfect your drop-in technique. Remember, you're hard-core now. Show some swagger, kook!

Beneath the Sand

The state of Florida sits atop a submerged platform of karst limestone, a geological shelf constructed from the skeletons of dead marine organisms—foraminifera, mollusks, echinoids, algae, and coral—who dropped their bones overtop the bones of the generations who came before them. This pileup of carbonate material runs 3 miles thick, a porous underwater mausoleum cut through by rivers, caves, sinkholes, and freshwater springs. The spiritually inclined might even imagine occult vibrations swimming through the latticework, the ghosts of creatures who respired and reproduced (and perhaps even dreamed) right here beneath our feet.

Archaeologists have dated humankind's arrival in Florida to about 15,000 years ago, at the tail end of the last glacial period. The Sunshine State was a couple hundred feet taller back then, and a hundred miles wider. Those first Pleistocene-epoch snowbirds would have tramped across a high, dry, grassy savanna and brushed shoulders with megafauna like giant ground sloths, woolly mammoths, and saber-toothed cats.

During epochs of global warmth, the Atlantic Ocean swallows up the whole of the peninsula. For ten or twenty thousand years, Florida sleeps at the bottom of a warm, shallow sea. When the earth cools down again, and the oceans recede, the Florida shelf resurfaces, shakes off its salty crust, and blossoms with terrestrial life. This cycle—up, down, submersed, exposed—repeats itself in an endless game of tidal peek-a-boo.

Right now, Florida is on its way back under. It happens. The inundation won't be particularly immediate or sudden. Anyone who has built a sandcastle at low tide understands how stray waves can come tickling at your castle walls for a good half hour before anything starts to crumble. Like those first tongues of water, the hurricanes and storm surges that

Ais children played on these beaches for 150 generations.

Rick Piper, *A Day at the Beach,* acrylic on canvas.

push up against Florida's foundations can be seen as forerunners of a rising tide.

Of all the world's landforms, none are more liminal, or subject to the whims of the sea, than barrier islands. Florida has 700 miles of them. They are sandbars, effectively—long, narrow accretions that mound up parallel to the coast—conveyed by longshore current and sculpted by waves and wind. On the island's foreshore (the sea-facing side), a system of dunes, carpeted with sea oats, acts a buffer against swells, dissipating the ocean's energy. To the leeward (between the island and the mainland), is a brackish waterway, a stillwater mangrove lagoon that sustains a menagerie of fish, seagrass, birds, cetaceans, and all manner of estuary biota.

When heavy winter waves or hurricane swells burst through the dunes, a tidal inlet opens up, blowing a "washover fan" of sand into the lagoon. One such rupture occurred about 2,000 years ago, near the heart of what is now downtown Cocoa Beach, at Minutemen Causeway. The eruptive flow from sea to river created a 900-acre bloom of shallow mangrove atolls known as the Thousand Islands.

The locals at the time were the Ais people, the dominant tribe on the east coast of Florida and brethren to the mighty Calusa, who ruled the Everglades and the swamps to the west. Ais territory included the 45 miles of palmetto scrub tapering down from Cape Canaveral to Sebastian Inlet, or what is modern-day Brevard County.

Elaborately pierced and tattooed, the Ais wore their hair in topknots, and stood as giants compared to the Europeans of the time. Their civilization can be traced back 4,000 years, to the age of the ancient Egyptians, and predated the Olmec, Maya, Inca, and Aztec.

They had survived enough cataclysmic storm surges to apprehend that beaches are temporal affairs, and that sand, like water, exists in a constant state of flux. Long periods of calm were consummated by apocalyptic floods. The island was folding back, migrating landward, generation after generation, a mutable border between land and sea, perpetually being erased and remade, like a sand painting. To adapt to this natural instability, the Ais built seasonally paired towns on either side of the river, retreating to the mainland when the shoreline was sloughed away, and rebuilding beachside when the white sands accrued again. So they existed for millennia, crossing and recrossing the river, making themselves as fluid as the sands.

For sheer bulk of water, no people on Earth were as immersed as these ancient Floridians. Water roiled and crested in the boundless east, it reflected in green labyrinthine mangroves, twisted through reedy estuaries and inlets, and strafed down at them from black thunderclouds. Water burbled up from cold springs, rilled over palmetto leaves, glistened on hibiscus petals and alligators' backs. It hung damp and heavy in the air they breathed and swelled from their every pore.

Only a habitat as wet as this could spawn an aquatic people like the Ais. Gliding like Tritons on their dugout canoes—hand-shaped vessels carved from slash pines, carefully stripped and hollowed out with fire and stone—they spearfished for stingrays and snook, and free-dove offshore bars to depths of 30 feet to harvest shellfish. The lagoon was clean and limpid in those days, pure-filtered by oyster reefs, lush with seagrass and glass minnows, and clear enough to sight pods of mullet and schools of 60-pound redfish from 100 yards away.

Scraps of Ais history have been exhumed from their burial mounds and oyster-shell middens. The colossal Turtle Mound—70 feet high and 600 feet wide—is the tallest midden in North America and looms today like an earthen pyramid over the New Smyrna wetlands. But other legends of the Ais can be gleaned only from eyewitness testimony and anecdotes transcribed by early European explorers. One of the most fantastical tales of Ais waterman prowess comes from the Jesuit missionary and naturalist José de Acosta, who, in *The Natural and Moral History of the Indies* (1590), recounts the Ais method of hunting right whales.

According to the Acosta account, when a whale is spotted off the coast, the Ais hunter launches an extralight offshore canoe into the surf, paddles out past the second sandbar, and draws up to the beast's side. When the whale breaches, the Ais leaps onto its neck and rides it as if on horseback, his muscles straining in the sunlight, and proceeds to thrust a sharp wooden stake into the whale's blowhole. All the while, the whale is bucking and lathering the sea, and spewing mountains of water. Then, with a great thunderclap of its fluke, it runs into the deep. Both whale and man disappear in a vortex of bubbles. How long are they under? Two minutes? Three? It hardly seems possible, but when they break through the surface again, the Ais youth is still clinging to the beast's neck! With a wild cry, he slams the second stake into the other nostril, fully plugging the blowhole. Now he impales a hook into the whale's flank, ties a rope to it, and swims back to his canoe. All that is left to do is to let the whale run, troll behind the suffocating monster as it thrashes and rolls, and row shoreward when the line goes slack. Once his catch is subdued, the Ais stalwart urges the whale into the breakwaters, where it washes up at the feet of the cheering masses. The spoils are gathered, the flesh cut into hunks that are dried and beaten into paste, and the feast commences.

I would find it difficult to believe such a seemingly spurious story had I not seen a right whale at close range some years ago. It was during a winter surf session, one of those solitary, glassy Cocoa Beach days at Thirteenth Street South. I was biding my time on the outside when I noticed a strange foaming of the water and what appeared to be an immense dorsal fin. But it was too big and too dark to be a dolphin's. Too big, even, to pass for the tip of one of those manta ray wings that sometimes grace the waterline. The top of it was slightly curled, nothing at all like a shark's. Nor was it rising and falling like a normal fin. Rather, it remained in place, and wiggled, as if waving to me. Suddenly, the sea around the fin creamed and lifted as one nacreous bulge, like an island emerging from below, and I finally understood what I was seeing—not a fin, but the pectoral flipper of a right whale.

But this gargantuan flipper, incredibly enough, belonged only to the *calf.* Below it, a 50-foot-long shadow, 100 tons of blubber and baleen, brewed in the depths like a submarine.

These right whales, the mother and calf, were swimming through the calmer, shallower nearshore waters on their yearly migration south. I kept my distance, maybe 60 yards or so (still uncomfortably close) spellbound by their mammoth, callus-encrusted snouts, the V-shaped blowholes, and the fountains of whistling steam.

What nerve must it have taken to vault onto a whale's back? And what power, what breath control, to hold fast to the sounding leviathan? Such was the spirit of the original dwellers of this fingerling barrier island. For 150 generations—more than twice the lifespan of the Roman Empire—Ais children played on these beaches, fished in this river, basked in the rose glow of these same sunsets, and listened to this very breeze crinkling through the sea grapes. And they might have gone on doing so for another four thousand years, had the European ships never reached these shores.

In April 1513, the Spanish conquistador Juan Ponce de León anchored three caravels on the east coast of Florida. The site of his landing, long assumed to be in the vicinity of Saint Augustine, has been recently challenged by a group of scholars, who relocated it to Melbourne Beach. The proponents of this Melbourne Beach landing theory even went so far as to erect a statue—a hideously deformed bronzework of the bearded Spaniard brandishing his cross out to sea—at one of the beach parking lots.

Juan Ponce de León is well known to all Floridian elementary schoolers for "discovering" and christening La Florida, and for his famous quest for the fountain of youth. Students are somewhat less familiar with Ponce de León's work as a slaver, and with the brutal atrocities he perpetuated on the Taíno people of Hispaniola. The butcheries are well documented: Bartolomé de Las Casas, a Dominican friar who joined the expedition in Hispaniola in 1504, wrote *A Short Account of the Destruction of the Indies,* in which he describes the massacres—the overrunning of cities, the "ripping up of bellies," the "dashing out the brains of innocent children on the rocks," the roasting of living men, the beheading of people for sport, and sundry other conquistadorian activities performed by Ponce de León and his men.

The Ais were better prepared than the Taíno, or perhaps forewarned, and not quite ready to be subjugated. Early skirmishes with the Spanish led to deaths on both sides and a tacit stalemate in which the Ais retained control over their land and the Spanish agreed to tread lightly (and build a fort here and there). In 1521, Ponce de León sailed around the Florida Keys and dropped anchor on the southwest coast of Florida, with the idea to establish a colony. The Calusa met him there and delivered some well-deserved karma in the form of a poisoned arrow.

One of the most detailed firsthand accounts of the Ais people comes from Jonathan Dickinson, a Quaker who shipwrecked in Florida in 1696. Dickinson was on his way from Jamaica to Philadelphia when a hurricane dashed his ships over the shoals and marooned the party on the barrier island. He was captured by the Ais, and brought to their capital city of Jece, on the north side of Sebastian Inlet. Dickinson's narrative (at times overburdened by effulgent praise for the Almighty, whom he thanks profusely and repetitively for his survival) details a fierce, thriving culture, their ritual dance ceremonies, and tells of their fearsome chief, the *Cacique,* who towered over the tribe in both body and mind, and who benevolently granted the interlopers passage up the "Rio de Ais."

As was the tragic case with most of the Indigenous peoples of the Americas, the Ais were bounded in on all sides, decimated by smallpox, and tyrannized by the explorers of the New World. The last of their kind died around 1760, their bones piled atop the never-ending heap.

For a time, the waterman spirit of this place was submerged. Ibises pecked among the dune daisies on the burial mounds. Oysters went unharvested. Waves peeled unridden on the outer sandbars. But some spectral energy of the Ais remained, a coiled life force beneath the surface, like sea-oat seeds shrouded by windblown sand.

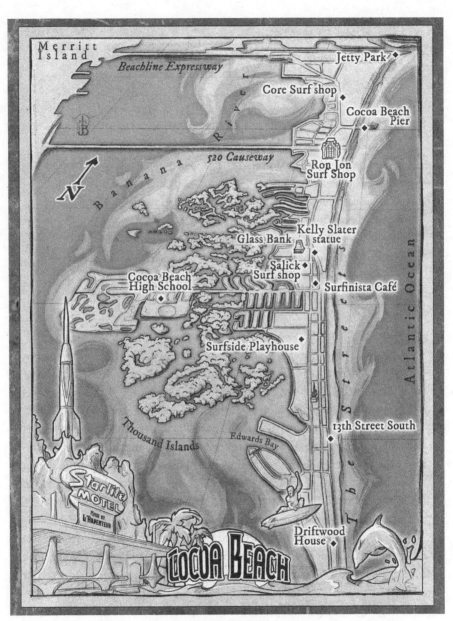

Cocoa Beach.

Illustration by Thibaud Jacquier-Bret.

The Golden Age

Around the turn of the twentieth century, before the barrier island was
moored to the mainland by bridges, a band of intrepid fishermen crossed
the Banana River and landed on a stretch of beach in the vicinity of the
modern-day Driftwood House, a place they called "Oceanus." They slashed
a path through the saw palmetto, trekked over the dunes, and looked out
on the waves. They sensed something, though they could not name it . . .
a power, a depth of energy, a profound and vital force awakening, as if
after a long slumber . . .

Any connoisseur of quality surf knows that Florida offers only slippery,
illusory prospects. Stir up a system out in the Atlantic and cast a long-
period fetch toward Brevard County, and it's a safe bet the waves will
combust in mile-long closeouts from Port Canaveral to Sebastian Inlet.
The sandbars are fickle and untrustworthy, the trade winds blow perpetually onshore, and a full tide tends to swallow anything under head-
high. Even when the west wind makes a cameo and the swell pushes in
at the perfect southwest angle, or when some fluke sandbar happens to
be doing its best impression of Rincon, the magic hour could well arrive
in the dead of night and dissipate like a vaporous dream in the morning.

All this gives the legend of Brevard County's first modern surf session
the ring of the apocryphal. It was the summer of 1959. Jack Murphy, a
Miami Beach hotel-dive-show rogue known to the surfing community
as Murf the Surf, and Dick Catri, a Neal Cassady–looking, cigarette-
smoking high-jump champion, headed up the coast from Miami, looking for waves. When they rolled into Indialantic, they were met with
offshore winds and blue-glass, head-high rollers breaking clean over the
outer sandbar and rifling all the way to the beach. Catri and Murphy
traced their elegant ogees on the outside, the Australian pines mur-
mured approval, and the golden age commenced.

Jack Murphy: East Coast surf champion, jewel thief, convicted murderer. Murphy (*left,* with John Eakes), circa 1961, more innocent times, in front of Brevard County's first surf shop, Indialantic.

Photograph courtesy of the Florida Surf Museum.

"We wound up staying a month in Brevard County," Catri recalled in a 2012 interview. "Between Indialantic and Cocoa Beach, we could find waves almost every day. It wasn't always big, but there were waves. And as soon as we got out of the water, everywhere we went there were always kids coming up and asking, 'Hey, can I rent your board?'"

Indialantic proved a low-action venue, but 15 miles to the north, the young scientists, engineers, and creative minds of the space race were flooding into Cocoa Beach, energized by their quest for manned space flight. Midcentury modern motels popped up all along State Road A1A. Rocket ships uncoiled in skeins of fire over the cape. Astronauts—John Glenn, Gus Grissom, and the fighter-jock heroes of Project Mercury— sped through town in gleaming Corvettes and tinkled cocktails with long-lashed, beehive-haired women at the Holiday Inn lounge.

It was the dawn of a new era, the era of the hot rod, of drive-in movies, of free love. And places like Cocoa Beach, low-lying strip towns with walk-right-in-your-room motels, did more to usher in the sexual revolution—as Tom Wolfe put it—than the pill.

Catri and Murphy had found their Shangri-la. They talked their way into jobs at the Starlite Motel, managing beach rentals, and began to shape surfboards out of one of the cabanas. In 1960, Catri (jaded, no doubt, by one of Florida's notorious flat spells) flew off to Hawaii. But Murphy remained in town and opened Brevard County's first surf shop, Murf's Surf Shop, in Indialantic. *Gidget* was still in theatrical release, and the towheaded children of the NASA workers shelled out cash as fast as Murphy could unpack the boards. Demand far outstripped supply, and, in the early '60s, Bill Feinberg started up Oceanside Surfboards, the first production shaping house in Brevard County, calling in California board builders Pat O'Hare and Johnny Rice to speed along the dream.

Warm water, beach access at the end of every street, sand bottoms, gentle waves . . . where else on the mainland could a kid spend more time in the surf than the Space Coast? Throw in the occasional hurricane swell and nor'easter to impart heavier lessons, and there might have been no better nursery for a budding surfer. Any kid willing to work the slop and finesse imperfect sections could catch 100 waves a day here, 300 days a year. So these towheads became water bugs, like the Ais before them.

The 1960s would produce Cocoa Beach's first modern youth movement: Bruce Valluzzi and Mike Tabeling of the Fifteenth Street crew, butter-smooth Claude Codgen, and a little white-haired punk named Gary Propper.

Gary Propper's fin-first takeoffs, supple heel-hangs, and Nureyevesque pivot turns earned him a reputation as one of the best surfers on the planet in conditions under 6 feet. Here's a young Propper, fully committed to a drop-knee cutback on a 1-foot wave.

Photograph courtesy of the Florida Surf Museum.

Florida's Mimi Munro is caught hugging the nose in a tight shore-break section during the finals at the Redondo Beach breakwater.

Mimi Munro, fourteen years old, ten toes over. Steering from the front, hand-dragging the lip, noseriding with intention and composure.

Photograph courtesy of the Florida Surf Museum.

In '64, Catri returned from his adventures in Hawaii—he'd surfed Sunset with Butch Van Artsdalen, Makaha with Buffalo Keaulana, and Pipeline a hundred times by himself—and signed on with Dick Brewer to distribute Surfboards Hawaii everywhere east of the Mississippi. Catri opened Satellite Surf Shop and scouted out the hottest local riders for his team. Valluzzi, Tabeling, Propper, and Fletcher Sharpe were his first disciples and, later, Joe and Betsy Twombly, Fred Grosskreutz, and twelve-year-old noseriding savant Mimi Munro. Catri's surf team would go on to sweep every contest on the East Coast and begin a forty-year tradition of competitive domination by Brevard County surfers.

Those were Technicolor, *I Dream of Jeannie* days. Chiffon headscarves, candy-colored surfboards, sunflower bikinis, Buick Skylarks in Teal Mist. From Ron Jon, that fledgling surf shop up on the Canaveral Pier,[1] speakers warbled the Ventures, Beach Boys, and Delltones out over the water. The pier was the center stage of East Coast surfing, and Propper—a whip-turning small-wave maestro—was its headliner. His fin-first takeoffs, supple heel-hangs, and Nureyevesque pivot turns earned

---

1   The Canaveral Pier, built in 1962 on the borderline between Cape Canaveral and Cocoa Beach, is now known as the Cocoa Beach Pier.

him a reputation as one of the best surfers on the planet in conditions under 6 feet. When Propper defeated Dewey Weber at the East Coast Surfing Championships in Virginia Beach in 1966, Hobie Alter recognized the potential of the brash kid as a surf star on the East Coast, and the Gary Propper Signature Model was born. It would become Hobie's best-selling surfboard of all time and make Propper the highest-paid surfer of his generation.

Ed Leasure—who owned and operated Quiet Flight Surf Shop in Cocoa Beach with his brother, Jim, for forty years—notes, "We had a high school graduating class of 87 people, and more top surfers than Huntington Beach, which has three schools of 1,000 students each. How is that possible?"

"We were just hungry," Tabeling said in a 2014 interview in *Surfer*. "We were eating, living, dreaming, dying for surf. We'd ride anything. California surfers didn't do that. Hawaiian surfers didn't do that."

The Canaveral Pier was center stage of the East Coast surf scene in the mid '60s. After a renovation in the '80s, it was renamed the Cocoa Beach Pier. The pier was one of the first breaks to come back to life after the dredging ruined the sandbars in 2005. Nowadays, when the tide is too high everywhere else, the "snack bar" wave on the pier's south side still peels off nicely.

Photograph courtesy of the Florida Surf Museum.

Catri, Codgen, and Valluzzi would surf in the Duke Invitational contest at Sunset Beach in 1967, garnering Florida a modicum of respect in Hawaii. Tabeling went off with Nat Young to ride for Weber, and traveled and surfed for years with Valluzzi in France, Spain, Portugal, and Morocco. Propper, uninterested in riding bigger waves, would glide out to Hollywood, hustle his way into the Teenage Mutant Ninja Turtles franchise, and make millions as a professional promoter.

One by one, the Cocoa Beach kids left their subtropical Eden. Some went off to war, others to Taylor Camp, a hippie commune in Kauai. Their hair deepened from blond to brown, their faces wrinkled like the sea under a turning wind. And just like that, the age of innocence, that golden summer of love, gave way to fall.

Youth Movement

~~~~~~

To fully understand Cocoa Beach, Florida, you must first be a child here. For those of us who came late—who weren't here yesterday, who never pedaled on spring-loaded legs up to the beach crossover, or jon-boated through the mangrove canals after school, or got trampled at the doors of the Surfside Playhouse[1] on opening night of *Five Summer Stories*—a fundamental secret lies forever across the Banana River, an unbridgeable gap between our perception of this place and the truth of it.

July 20, 1969: The children of Cocoa Beach tilted their freckled faces to the northern sky and stood up an inch taller on their toes. They watched as the Saturn V rocket, dream child of their fathers, burned into the upper reaches of the stratosphere. When the first stage exploded and dropped away, and the ship got smaller and faster and farther out, they understood it to mean more speed, more altitude, more freedom . . . for some of them had been experimenting with this very same concept—this paring of the vessel—in their own garages.

"We were getting rid of the board. Trimming it down," says Pete Dooley, who was one of the first shapers in Cocoa Beach to subscribe to the thought experiments of Greenough and Weber[2] and slice the noses off his longboards. Dooley started shaping surfboards in the late '60s out of a Visqueen-and-cardboard lean-to at Sixteenth Street, but soon built himself a real shaping bay and founded Natural Art Surfboards. Natural Art would go on to produce more than forty thousand light-

---

1 Built in 1963 on Brevard Avenue and Fifth Street South, the Surfside Playhouse, Cocoa Beach's community theater, regularly overflows its capacity when it screens surf movies.

2 George Greenough and Dewey Weber: two of the architects of the shortboard revolution.

weight crafts in variegated airbrush and neon-bladed flourishes for the surfers of the '70s, '80s, and '90s. "The generation before us, they rode a board on a wave," Dooley remarks. "We rode the wave."

The *Beach Blanket Bingo* shit was over. The revolution was on. Suddenly, the unmakeable shorepounds of Patrick Air Force Base, Satellite Beach, and Melbourne Beach had transmogrified into racy walls and workable barrels. The surfers migrated south like a flock of black-winged gulls in their Chevelles and El Caminos. Soon, a crew of Cocoa Beach locals—Tabeling, Valluzzi, Larry Pope, and the Salick brothers—discovered a hidden treasure at Sebastian Inlet. The recently reconstructed jetty (another high concept of government engineers) was consistently ricocheting a bounce-back wave into the incoming swell, producing a powerful, steep, double-up peak twice as fast and twice as big as anywhere else in the county.

Phil Salick—whose identical-twin brother, Rich, was the father of Philip, that beauty boy from my Topanga Canyon commune days—remembers those halcyon years at Sebastian. "We had a decade where only 15 of us were surfing the inlet," he says. But the radical wave at First Peak,[3] progeny of the technological age, proved too photogenic to remain a secret for long. A shot of Tabeling wrapping a cutback there made the cover of *Surfer* in 1971, and the locusts descended the morning after the issue hit newsstands.

This posed an unfamiliar dilemma for the Florida surfers, with the Peak having a single takeoff zone and a hundred heads in the water. It was a recipe for a bloodbath, and it gave rise to a savage pecking order. Jeff Crawford, a tube-riding, hotheaded goofyfooter from Titusville, became First Peak's de facto enforcer. He banished nuisance surfers to Second Peak, 75 yards down the beach, threatening them with spankings or simply paddling over their backs, fins and all. "Somebody's gotta be the lifeguard," Crawford reasons. "And I saved a lotta souls from getting lost."

"Localism, it happened at the inlet," admits Greg Loehr, the high prince of the early Ocean Avenue crew. Ocean Avenue, the Melbourne Beach surf and skate team founded by Lewis Graves and Bruce Walker,

---

3 At point breaks, the "first peak" refers to the prominent takeoff zone, where the main wave begins to break. Sebastian's First Peak is a right-hander that jacks up against the jetty and produces the steepest, hollowest, and most coveted section of the wave.

reigned supreme at the inlet through the '70s. "There was this X in the water where you had to be," Loehr says. "And we knew where the X was. Not too many other people did. And we were protective of it."

The speed, the drop, the fight-your-way-in mentality: Sebastian Inlet had scaled-down affinities with the North Shore of Oahu. Earn your respect, and the apex surfers get their waves. This education in aggression, this jockeying and hassling, would serve Loehr and Crawford well in the lineups at Sunset and Pipeline. In 1974, Crawford was invited to surf in the Pipeline Masters (surfing's most prestigious contest at its most storied wave). A freak bomb swung his way right out the gate, and he ensorcelled his 8'2" pintail into a six-second vanishing act. It was enough to beat Gerry Lopez and Rory Russell and become the first Florida boy to win the event. (He wouldn't be the last.) "They had very little respect for East Coast surfers back then," Crawford says.

When they heard the news of Crawford's victory, the children of Cocoa Beach, who had watched Lopez win the event on *Wide World of Sports* the year before, grew another inch, and swelled with more pride than they had for any old moon landing.

By 1975, the Apollo blueprints were rolled up and packed away, the launchpads decommissioned, and many of Cocoa Beach's best and brightest had loaded their station wagons and ridden on to greener pastures. Housing prices tumbled, and the town drifted into a seedy, frayed, run-down, heavy-drinking shell of itself. The motel signs collapsed and lay burned-out and rusted on the ground, and the once-lustrous symbols of the future littered the streets like so many broken children's toys.

Even the fabled patriarchs fell on hard times. Dick Catri got punched for selling weed and served five months, and Jack Murphy, who famously scaled the walls of the New York Museum of Natural History back in '64—pulling off a glamorous heist of the Star of India, one of the world's largest sapphires—had turned to darker, more sinister deeds and was serving a life sentence for murder.

Many of the hard-core surfers were involved in some way in the drug trade. The Salick brothers, who opened up Salick Surf Shop on Third Street North in Cocoa Beach, knew all the smugglers on both coasts of Florida and saw the surfboards coming in from Morocco with 6-inch-wide stringers made of pure hash. Phil Salick shakes his head when the subject of Jack Murphy comes up. "Murf fucked up royal," he says. "It was not good."

But the sins of the fathers were not the sins of the children. The mid-century motel swimming pools had been drained, and new realms were opening in the empty shells. Kryptonics came out with urethane skateboard wheels in 1976, a significant improvement over Cadillac wheels, and the local kids began doing some of the first progressive pool skateboarding at Pool and Palms between Sixth and Seventh Streets.

Matt Kechele, curly-headed cherub of Cocoa Beach, grew up 100 yards from the Salick brothers' shop, skidded his bike tires all over the ramshackle town, got mauled at the doors of the Surfside Playhouse, and surfed his home break in front of a little burger shack on the beach called the Islander Hut. By the age of thirteen, Kechele was hitching rides to Sebastian Inlet, where he remembers his mind being blown by Loehr's skateboard-inspired lines at First Peak.

"Grinding on the lip, getting the fins out the back," Kechele says. "In the pool, you'd go up and tap your tail on the coping, then straight back down. Greg Loehr was doing that in the water. He was getting his board straight up to 12 o'clock, then pivoting it. That's all we wanted to do. Get vertical, get your chin up where it's touching your knee, straight up and down, whether frontside or backside, and then pivot."

It wasn't long before Bruce Walker caught sight of what looked like a beam of sunlight streaking across the face of a Second Peak left, slashing windblown plumes of whitewater in the air. It was a fifteen-year-old Kechele, brazenly defying the concept of friction. Walker immediately invited him to join their ranks. "Ocean Avenue was halfway to Sebastian," Kechele says. "If I could just get to the shop, I could get to the inlet. They were the most progressive thing on the East Coast. Champion surfers. Champion skateboarders. Nothing but raw progression. Everybody feeding off each other."

Walker remembers those sessions that erupted in late '78 and early '79: Amped on Devo, looking to push the limits, the crew would hit the water like a team of pack animals. "Every day, the team rode down to the inlet in the Ocean Avenue van," he says. "Jeff Klugel, Matt Kechele, Greg Taylor, Tony Graham, Tim Briers. It didn't matter if it was 1 to 2 feet. It was psychotic."

In 1978, Darryl Bulger, who was shaping for Mark Richards in Australia, brought one of his twin-fins to Brevard County and got it into Loehr's hands. Klugel was the first to ride it, and when the Ocean Avenue team saw how much faster he was going, the single-fins began to hit the scrap heap. Loehr, who'd learned to mow foam from Owl Chapman in Hawaii, started shaping twins for Klugel and Kechele, experimenting with thinner, narrower boards and adding slight concaves in the bottoms to better cleave the surface and accelerate through the bottom turns.

At the same time, a skateboarder down in South Florida, Alan Gelfand, was working out the trial phases of a new trick: the ollie pop. Gelfand had accidentally stumbled upon it—he would pop his board up over the edge of the wooden lip of a ramp, then transition in the air with no hands and ride back down. Kechele became fixated on the notion of transposing the ollie onto the wedge section at the inlet: gather speed, lift off, pivot with no rail grab, land, and ride on through. Why not?

Loehr and Kechele—both sons of aerospace engineers—took a scientific approach to designing a surfboard that would accomplish something surfboards had never before been made to do: *fly*. They tweaked the templates, tested flamboyant iterations. "The inlet was our laboratory," Loehr says. They arrived finally at a design called the Kech Air, a twin-fin squashtail that mimicked the outline of a skateboard, maximized speed, and allowed for a tail release.

By the spring of '79, Kechele was routinely executing functional, flow-driven aerials. While California aerial pioneers like Davey Smith, the McClure brothers, and Kevin Reed had already broken free of the lip, no one on Earth was launching and landing them like Kechele. These groundbreaking boosts—first by Kechele and then by Satellite Beach local John Holeman, who was sticking full 360 airs in 1981—predated Christian Fletcher's iconic flights by five years.

Kechele would follow in the footsteps of Catri, Codgen, Loehr, and Crawford, first to Hawaii and then onward to the World Tour. Meanwhile, back in Cocoa Beach, new legends were emerging. A group of ultra-groms were attaining otherworldly speed on the inside waves at Third Street North, right there in front of the Islander Hut.

Kechele recalls his first time seeing Kelly Slater, by far the tiniest surfer in the water: "It was incredible. I saw him do three backside 360s on this boogie board with fins. I think it was called a tubo. Really weird, super flexy, and thick."

The Ais leaps onto the whale. Neil Armstrong blasts off into the heavens. Matt Kechele levitates. Kelly Slater generates impossible speed on mushy, gutless surf, draws his own power from thin air. Echoes of Olympus resound throughout the mythology of Cocoa Beach. As when Dick

Catri, by that time sporting his white sea-captain's beard and looking something like Zeus, stood in front of the Islander Hut, arms crossed, cast his eye upon the child sensations of Third Street North—Kelly and Sean Slater, Todd Holland, Sean O'Hare, Troy Propper, Scott Bouchard—and decided to field a next-generation team of competitive surfers.

"Dick figured out pretty fast that he could stack a division like ours," says O'Hare, son of Pat O'Hare, who shaped all of Greg Noll's East Coast boards back in the '60s. "Boys and menehunes. We would place first through fifth and be in contention to win the team event. Dick kinda worked the system a little bit. He was bringing us up, trying to make us into better surfers."

"We would have workouts every weekend," Catri said. "I would put four of them in the water at a time, have the rest of the team sitting on the beach judging."

Catri ran practices out of his new surf shop, Shagg's, in Melbourne Beach, had the kids do calisthenics on the beach, and introduced them to Peter Townend and Ian Cairns when the Bronzed Aussies were in town for the Florida Pro.

"We'd go see him every other Sunday and he would go over technique," Slater says. "A couple mock heats here and there. How to look at the wave in a certain way. Catri would say, 'Instead of taking off at the peak, how about you fade back there, and that's part of the art of the ride.' I remember surfing the shorebreak behind his house one time, barreling little tubes, and he goes, 'When you're in those tubes do you have your eyes open? Open your fucking eyes.' There were a few little bits of gold he told us. He planted a lot of seeds."

The Cocoa Beach kids learned to work hard, to squeeze all the juice out of the orange. In 1981, they traveled up the coast and plundered prize money and trophies like mercenaries. It was a triumph, a curtain call for the Godfather of East Coast surfing—Coach Catri—who would retire from the contest scene the following season. "Kelly got invited to surf with Matt Kechele," Catri said. "Todd Holland went with Pete Dooley and Natural Art. I went and got my captain's license and made that a profession."

Holland, a cocky little hurricane in the tradition of Propper or Crawford and a balls-of-steel teenage charger at Pipe, Sunset, and Waimea, became the youngest surfer ever on the national team. Slater, meanwhile, would hang back on the East Coast, watching and learning from

Holland's pro success, crushing the amateur circuit, riding Kechele-shaped boards, and honing his skills at the inlet alongside world-class talent like Bill Hartley, Dave Speir, and Pat Mulhern.

The rest of the Kelly Slater story is well known and well told: star child of Cocoa Beach, culmination of watermen epochs, improvises, reacts, anticipates the water better than anyone on Earth, takes aerials and ac-robatic surfing into the mainstream as the leader of the New School. Ascends into the collective consciousness. Blows the tail out in contest heats, takes chances no one else dreams of. *Kelly Slater in Black & White.* *Momentum. Baywatch.* Pamela Anderson. Eight Pipeline Masters. Eleven world titles. Enkindling hyperbole the world over, Slater would afford Florida permanent credibility in the surfing universe.

"It all came from mastering small waves," Kechele remarks.

Passages from the Surfer's Bible

This comic piece, first published more than ten years ago in the *Beachside Resident,* was recently resurrected by the Florida Surf Museum. Despite its irreverent take on the Good Book, the museum people tell me it has become one of their most popular exhibits.

Genesis 1:1

In the beginning, God created the seas. And the Spirit of God hovered over the face of the waters. And when the Lord saw that the waters were without form, He said, "Let there be waves," and there were waves. Then, seeing that the waves were good—indeed they were very good—the Lord God took the rest of the day off.

Genesis 2:8

The Lord God planted some islands eastward in the Pacific, and upon every reef and bay he made the waters to rise and peel away in clean points. And the winds blew pleasantly offshore all the day long, so that the waves were ideal for riding. And God created the Ancient Hawaiians to inhabit His islands, to tend and keep them. And the Lord God commanded them, saying, "Every wave of these islands you may freely surf, only I command you, do not *snake*[1] each other."

Genesis 5:1

When Duke was 204 years old, he begat Blake, who lived to be 117, and Blake begat Simmons. And all the days of Simmons were 340 years. And Simmons begat Edwards, who lived to 122, and Edwards begat Dora . . .

---

1 Snake: "Snaking," or "burning," happens when one surfer, ignoring the rules of surf etiquette, illicitly paddles behind another one and steals their wave.

Genesis 6:1

Now it came to pass, when men began to multiply on the face of oceans, especially in Southern California, that God saw the great wickedness of surfers, whose every intent and thought of their hearts was only evil continually. And the Lord was dismayed He had filled the lineups so, and He said, "I will destroy these surfers whom I have created, for I am sorry I have made so many of them." And He cast a terrible flatness over the whole of the seas, and drove them all inland, to the Valley.

Genesis 22:1

After Dora had been on the Ha'ena coast two years, God tested him. He said, "Dora! Take your board, your only Da Cat model which you love with all your heart, and offer it as a burnt sacrifice up on the mountain." So Dora rose early in the morning, and he split the wood for the burnt offering, and went with his board up to the mountain. And Dora built an altar there and placed the wood in order; and he bound his only surfboard on the altar upon the wood. But the Angel of the Lord called to him from heaven and said, "Dora! Do not lay your hand on that board, for I know now that you believe in Me." Then Dora lifted his eyes, and over the cliffs a lofty set came billowing in from the north.

Exodus 7:17–11:9 (The Plagues)

I. Red tide

"I will strike the water, and it shall be turned to blood. The fish shall die, the sea itself shall stink, and the throats and eyes of the surfers shall burn as with fire."

II. Medusas

"The ocean shall swarm with jellyfish; they shall froth and writhe upon all your people."

III. Lice

"And all seaweed of the seas shall become infested with lice."

IV. Kooks

"I shall send swarms of kooks upon you, upon your secret spots, so that they shall form an unbroken line across the beach."

V. Sewage

"A deadly pestilence shall leak out from the bowels of the cities, and contaminate all the seas."

VI. Fat, Pasty Children in Rubber Rings

"And great hordes of fat, pasty children in rubber rings shall float in the shorebreak so as to thwart your people from the plentiful inside barrels of the high tide."

VII. Onshores

"And the seas shall foment, and the onshore winds shall batter the coast day and night without respite."

VIII. Hammerheads

"And I will bring blunt-headed sharks into your country. They shall fill the sea and devour the last remnant of you in the water after the onshores."

IX. Boils

"And I will make the sun to burn your flesh, so that boils come up on the surface of your skin."

X. The Final Plague

"And finally, I shall groom the waters, and blow the winds favorably, so that you shall be tempted out. And thenceforth I shall bring upon you sweepers,[2] great hordes of sweepers like a forest upon the surface of the sea."

I Kings 3:16

Two men came to the king and stood before him, and the first said, "Please, my lord, this dude and I surf the same break; and when I was checking the waves, he ganked my board from my car." But the second surfer said, "No, the board is mine!" And so they argued before the king. Then the king told his servant, "Bring me a sword. Now divide the board in two; we will give half to the one, and half to the other." But the first surfer, who loved the board, said to the king, "Please, my lord, it is a local

---

2   Sweepers: stand-up paddleboarders.

handmade shape! Let him take the board; do not cut it!" And the king answered verily, "Give the board to this dude, here, and in no ways split it. He is the rightful owner."

Psalm 1

Happy are those who do not drift along with crowds, for their delight is the solitude of the waves. Their faith needs not the affirmation of others.

Psalm 23

The Lord is my shepherd; I shall not want. He makes me tuck into green barrels; he leads me out through calm channels. He restores my soul; he lifts me across steep faces and engages my rail in His name.

Psalm 29

Do not be afraid when some become rich, for when they die they will carry nothing away. Concern yourself not with wealth, but with the wind and the 20-mile buoy.

Proverbs 9:7

Whoever tries to regulate wins abuse; a kook will only hate you for it. The wise, when regulated, will heed you. Give instruction to the wise, and they shall become wiser still.

Proverbs 11:1

Chop hopping is an abomination to the Lord; smoothness is his delight. All those who check their spray invite disgrace.

Matthew 5:5

Blessed are the groms,[3] for they shall inherit the waves.

Matthew 5:22

"But I say to you that if you paddle out at a local break you will be liable to judgment; and if you drop in on someone you will be liable to the hell of fire."

---

3 Grom (grommet, gremmie): a young surfer, typically under the age of fourteen.

"The Lord God shall finish His work tomorrow."

Illustration © John Klossner. www.jklossner.com.

Matthew 6:19

Lay not up for yourselves treasures upon earth, where moth and rust doth corrupt, and where thieves break through and steal:

But lay up for yourselves treasures in the water:

For where your treasure is, there will your heart be also.

Matthew 6:24

No one can serve two masters. Either he will hate the one and love the other, or he will be devoted to the one and despise the other. You cannot serve both Surfing and your Day Job.

Matthew 16:26

What good does it serve a man who discovers a secret sandbar, but brings no board with him?

Matthew 22:27

"Love the Lord your God with all your heart and with all your soul and with all your mind." This is the first and greatest commandment. And the second is like it: "Love the sponger[4] as yourself."

Revelation 5:8

When Slater had taken the trophy, the three finalists and the twenty-four competitors fell before him, each holding golden bowls full of incense. And his radiance was like a very rare jewel, like a jasper, clear as crystal.

---

4 Sponger: boogie boarder.

Juracán

The Taíno people of the Antilles worshipped *zemis,* gods of storm, fire, earthquake, and flood, who formed and transfigured the mountains, coves, and cascading rivers of their island world. The wildest and most capricious of these deities was Guabancex—mother of chaos, disaster, sacred rage, and transformation. When the goddess grew angry with her subjects, she would conjure *juracán,* the all-destroying tempest, and set its merciless, spiraling winds loose upon the earth.

Mayan lore also spoke of Huracán, their god of wind and storm, who called forth the Great Flood, drowned the universe, killed the second generation of gods, and enjoined the earth to regenerate from the ruins.

The flood legend is as least as old as literature itself. Civilization-consuming storms appear in tales as far back as the Mesopotamian *Epic of Gilgamesh.* The ancient Greeks told of Deucalion, a precursor to Noah, who built his ark and moored it atop Mount Parnassus to wait out the tides. In Aztec tradition, a Great Flood ravaged the human race, only instead of drowning everyone, it turned them all into fish.

Flood myths read like morality plays; in every one of them, the people vex the gods and are dealt punishment by water. The storm is a portent, a message, a violent alembic come to wash away their sins.

To live under specter of hurricane is to deal with the fact that humans are essentially helpless creatures, subjects to the whims of the skies. In a place where two-hundred-year-old grandfather oaks can be casually ripped root-over-branch by invisible spirits, and where one's walls and roof are occasionally blasted to splinters and cast downstream, the instinct is to attribute some meaning to these random takedowns.

How else can we do this but by telling ourselves stories?

In Florida, every *juracán* is a story.

The Halloween Swell, 1991

Only one tribe in the history of mankind has ever glorified the hurricane as a beneficent force and summoned it with prayers and supplications. The legends of this audacious people diverge from flood myths of old: in their telling, *juracán* is not dealt as retribution for the iniquities of the people; rather, it manifests as a reward for their patience and faith during the spare, waveless months of summer. These are the surfers of Florida, and the hurricane is embedded in their rituals and vernacular.

The very names of storms conjure religious iconography. Irma: Radiant Mother. Hugo: Sun God. Bertha: Bountiful Queen. A Florida surfer's gaze will go far off and a wistful smile will play on his lips when he speaks their names out loud. "Joaquin. Gave us two weeks of nonstop swell. Every day we surfed down at Driftwood House. It was like blue corduroy, man. Head-high glass . . ." His voice will trail off as he loses himself in meditative visions of steep, shimmering takeoffs, blinding spray, ramps of blue mirrorglass.

It goes without saying that the holiest of their hurricanes are not the ones that make landfall, but those storms that steamroll through the Sargasso, then veer north and stall in that exalted crescent of Atlantic between Bermuda and Nova Scotia, where they roil up the deepwater currents and produce the fabled wave events so fundamental to devotees of the faith.

Of all the hurricane swell tales told by this tribe, none is more sacred or awe-inspiring than the Halloween Swell of 1991.

It originated on October 26, with the formation of a minor, late-season storm, Hurricane Grace, an inconsequential Category 2 on the Saffir-Simpson scale that posed no threat to Florida, as its westward progress was halted over Bermuda by a prodigious nor'easter that was battering the East Coast and blowing into the Atlantic.

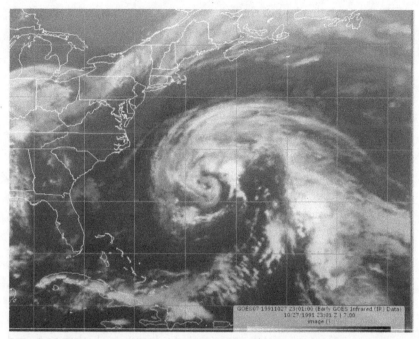

The Perfect Storm, October 27, 1991. Vapor imagery of Hurricane Grace emulating a gigantic, pitching wave. Note the Arctic high-pressure system compressing the leading edge of the storm. Once-in-a-generation conditions for swell propagation.

NOAA satellite image.

On October 28, the leading edge of Hurricane Grace collided with the cold, nameless nor'easter, and a whirling dance of fire and ice commenced. The extreme convective energies of the combined tempest (later dubbed the "Perfect Storm") would spiral in place for three days, setting off a historical wave-building event. While the sustained winds at the heart of the storm measured only 70–80 miles per hour (slightly less than tropical-force wind speeds), the persistence and geographic scope of the blow was historic. On October 30, an offshore buoy south of Halifax recorded a wave height of 100.7 feet. This was, and still is, the largest wave on record in all of the Scotian Shelf. By the time the nor'easter had fully absorbed the tropical cyclone, the impact zone of the storm would measure more than 1,200 miles in diameter.

Down in Florida, surfers listened to weather radio and waited on the edge of their couches for the meteorologist to come on the six o'clock news. The satellite image was breathtaking. Grace was being sucked into the high circulating belt of the nor'easter, fraying apart, and reconfiguring as a whirling, eyeless ghost in the central vortex of the storm.

A storm of this magnitude, spinning in that cauldron between Cape Cod and Cape Hatteras, could not fail to hurl a swell of epic proportions toward their beaches. It would take a day or two for the waves to make their way down from the North. What happened next was anyone's guess.

Matt Kechele—one of the few people in the state capable of predicting *and* riding these sudden-onset XXL waves—was in a better position to guess than most. He'd recently returned home to Florida from a stint on the world tour and had become a celebrity among the hard-core Sebastian Inlet locals. An aerial pioneer in the late '70s, one of the old-school Ocean Avenue crew, an early mentor to Kelly Slater, and a shaper with his own eponymous line of surfboards, Kech was now a wily veteran, still sharp as ever, and famous of late for putting himself in exactly the right place at the right time, be it Reef Road in Palm Beach, or Puerto Rico on a giant north-tilt winter swell.

Chasing hurricanes on the East Coast requires an intimacy with buoy readings, wind vectors, fetch, wave periods, deepwater bathymetry, and ever-shifting sandbar configurations. Swell windows in Florida are typically short and tidal-dependent, and local winds are always an X factor. You need to be able to read the tea leaves.

An electric current still pulses through Kechele's voice when he talks about the Halloween Swell, even now, thirty-three years later: "Those true north swells are rare," he tells me. "And a storm of that size. The weather forecasters were really hyping it, with good reason. They could see how those two frontal boundaries were going to join up. The gradients aligned, and the two storms combined. It was monstrous. When we started looking at the wave charts, the size of the waves, we'd never seen it like that before."

On Halloween morning, the barrier island awoke trembling and rattling from the concussions, as loud a cannonade from the sea as anyone had ever heard before. Overnight, the wind had switched out of the west, lacquering the water's surface. The inside sets, crushing green-and-white guillotines, looked to be triple overhead. Avalanche after avalanche thundered all the way back to the horizon. From up on the dune crossover, gazing over the whitecaps, there was no way to assess how big the waves were on the outside.

The easiest way to apprehend the size of an ocean wave is to measure its height as taken from trough to crest. Another, arguably more important, factor in determining a wave's size is its period—the amount of time it takes two successive waves to pass the same point. A longer-period wave means it has journeyed longer over open ocean, and its troughs and peaks have spread farther apart. Longer-period wave energy runs deeper; these waves travel faster, with more kinetic energy and momentum. They also surge higher, and break more powerfully upon reaching shallow waters. Florida surfers can formulate a crude estimate of how big a wave will be when it crashes on the shore by multiplying the wave's height by its period, then dividing the product by ten. For example: a 5-foot wave with an 8-second period would translate roughly to a 4-foot wave on the beach. This calculation method is fairly effective on short-period wind swells, but for longer-period ground swells (anything more than 10 seconds), the wave size is amplified. The formation of the sea floor and tidal effects play in as well, but the math falls apart on higher period swells. A 4-foot groundswell with a 14-second period, for example, has the potential to jack up into a 10-foot beast, given the right conditions.

By midday on Halloween, the 20-mile buoy east of Cape Canaveral was registering a wave height of 18.4 feet with a period of 20 seconds.

There are no easy paddle-outs on big Florida days, no point breaks to divert the wave energy, no key-hole channels to slide through. Only elite watermen can fight past the midbreak when it's double overhead. Halloween Day presented a next-level scale of difficulty.

But Kechele and his crew were keen to try. Among them were Todd Morcom, Paul Reineke, Bill Hartley, Scott Bouchard, Dave Speir, Jeff Klugel, Charlie Kuhn, and Rich Rudolph. Most had already tackled gigantic Hawaiian swells as teenagers. If they could just get to the outside, they knew they could ride these waves, whatever the size. But the drift was raging to the north, and by the time they made it out, they had been sucked nearly a mile up the beach.

"It was taking us about forty-five minutes to get outside," Kechele says. "It was pretty crazy. We were all in a kinda little group at RC's, sitting way out farther than we'd ever sat, and we were all just chuckling, you know, couldn't believe it. What's going on? These big outer reef sets, big whitewaters rolling through. It was bizarre, I gotta tell you, for around here."

By afternoon, the crew had it wired. Kevin Welsh, director of *Surf NRG*, a VHS-era East Coast surf production, captured video of that mythic Halloween session at RC's. In the grainy footage, Todd Morcom and Paul Reineke rise out of the silver air like tiny water spiders, flitting across the face of a shape-shifting colossus, cleaving a 20-foot warbling, darkening wall. Morcom drives hard to the bottom as Reineke flies up and gouges the lip. Now Reineke cuts back, Morcom elevates, and they switch places, hurling their boards like rapiers, playing around like groms on a head-high day at the pier. On another wave, Jeff Klugel swings into a ragged, warping right that might easily pass for Backdoor Pipeline on a big winter day.

"Later on, the tide started going out," Kechele says. "And I started catching these waves that were super far out, probably three-quarters of a mile out to sea. I had a Waimea board, a 9'4" gun. It was pretty rad. Triple overhead, probably bigger—the faces. They were big, rolling swells out there. It was perking up at this one spot, an outer reef, wedging up. You could get an exciting drop, then come off the bottom, do a nice little cutback, then it would get fat and you could kick out. They call 'em bombies. Like an outer bombie wave. Really fun, for around here. Probably we'll never see it again."

Most Floridians would be hard-pressed to fathom the peculiar type of insanity that could compel someone to launch themselves into the sea during the nightmarish conditions of Halloween Day, 1991. From the beach, it would look very much like a suicide run. Had anyone been watching, or trying to watch, those sessions that went down that day, they would have assumed the surfers to be lost, as they were out too far to be seen with the naked eye.

Hurricane season vibrates with the steady hum of existential angst. At any moment, a storm might leap out of the wings, flood the cities, demolish the homes, and cast the people into watery graves. But that peculiar tribe on the East Coast of Florida—made ravenous by months of hot, flat, surfless days—scorn the risks, lie in wait, and pray for the *zemis* to hatch.

Frances and Jeanne, 2004

~~~~~~~~~~~~~~~~

It may be a coincidence, though I doubt it somehow, but the same year I became addicted to surfing, I fell in love. Brittany was a student at the University of South Florida, nineteen, a Lakeland girl with a southern accent, exactly what I'd imagine a Scottish princess to look like. She was a good sport, too, and rode out with me from Tampa to Cocoa Beach every weekend, learned to surf, even picked up a used 7'8" Kechele wide-body board off the rack at the Longboard House (she liked the playing-card spade "K" logo) and joined me in my ablutions.

It didn't matter what the ocean looked like. All we had to do was snap up the boards from the apartment and dash across A1A. Cocoa Beach was glorious that way—waves beckoned at the end of every street. We paddled out any time, in any conditions. We were kooks, or semi-kooks, but even an hour-long struggle in the worst sideshore slop offered transformative moments, those tiny slippages of consciousness that guided our progression as surfers.

We experimented with takeoff angles, clung to higher and higher lines, gained balance and intuition with every session. We were learning to flow, together, unconsciously emulating the classic style of the locals—those salty, bearded Cocoa Beach noseriding masters.

When the wind was offshore and the surf was hitting, Cocoa Beach's parking lots would be packed with cars and surfers. But the less-than-perfect days were better in many ways, mellower, populated only by locals, the sun-baked, long-haired, everyday crew, slinging their longboards on beach cruisers, communing with each other with nods and knowing shakas.

We chatted on the beach crossovers with the wind-kissed gentry: electricians, yoga teachers, retired lawyers who'd grown out their freak flags, beachside teens skipping school, barefoot metaphysicists . . . the stoked, the hungry, and the well-leathered, hanging over the wooden rails to scope the waves. The town moved with a perpetual Sunday-morning rhythm, and we began to feel like part of the community—*insiders.*

In California, a fierce sense of ownership accompanies every perfectly peeling point break wave, but in Cocoa Beach, and especially at "the Streets," the surfers are open-hearted and generous in a way you don't see out west. This attitude derives naturally from the mediocre, short-period waves, and the fact that there are plenty of sandbars to go around.

I was twenty-five when I asked Brittany to marry me. I could hear her heart thumping outside of her chest. She wanted to know if I was serious. I was holding a flower instead of a ring. I said I was.

I realized about the same time that in order to maintain a serious surfing habit, I would need to spend more than just weekends at the roach-trap apartment on Fifth Street. The traffic jams from Tampa were getting to be soul-fraying, especially when the surf was on. By this time, I'd saved enough money from my construction work to put a down payment on a modest house in Cocoa Beach, a fixer-upper on Eleventh Street, two blocks from the beach and two blocks from the river.

It was a low-slung, sturdy, concrete-block job, originally built in 1959 for one of the young aerospace engineers of Project Mercury. Two bedrooms, two bathrooms, 1,200 square feet, with clean, simple midcentury lines and petal-patterned breeze blocks on the front facade. The soffits were so rotten you could jam your thumb through the wood, and when you opened the front door, a wall stood right there in front of you, blocking your sight line. The popcorn ceilings had been caramelized from decades of cigarette smoke absorption. One of the previous owners had recklessly tacked carpet over the terrazzo, and the 1970s floral-print furniture reeked with the antiseptic musk of mothballs. But the backyard was spacious, and it would be easy enough to knock down the offending wall and repaint the ceilings. Anyway, it was home. We had a deed and a boundary survey to prove it. Our little plot in heaven: $180,000 all told, and only a five-minute walk to the beach.

We hacked out the old windows, scraped up the linoleum, laid down oak floors, finish-nailed, puttied, and caulked the trim. We banged and sawed through the night, rolled and rerolled the ceilings with white paint like those obliviously happy children painting the fence in *Tom Sawyer.* By June, we had the carpets and furniture jettisoned, the rooms aired out, the interior walls painted a pale periwinkle, the exterior walls a seafoam green, and the kitchen fitted with new appliances and blue-pearl granite tops. We hung the walls with original artwork by a local Cocoa Beach artist, Rick Piper—surrealist ocean scenes of bent horizons, carnival-mirror sunsets, shafts of light almost too bright to look at directly, and pods of mullet speeding below the surface. Piper's handling of water seemed to capture the essence of what it meant to live here on the barrier island.

All this is to say, we were settling in, making ourselves comfortable.

———

Hurricane season in Florida runs from the first of June through the end of November. Half a year long, every year. As a kid in South Florida, in 1992, I'd ridden out Hurricane Andrew. I'd seen our windows blown out and watched the neighborhood trees snap like twigs, but that was more than twenty years ago, and hurricane seasons had been mostly quiescent since. Two decades of El Niño had kept the storms at bay, and Floridians had grown complacent. Hurricanes seemed to us dangerous rarities, about as likely to claim any of us as lightning strikes or shark attacks.

Our neighbors, Mary and Maurice, a kindly old couple with *Leave It to Beaver* inflections and '80s-style tracksuits, had lived in their house since 1954 and were convinced that Cocoa Beach was magically shielded from hurricane strikes. They backed up this conviction with the unimpeachable fact that no major hurricane had struck the area in the past fifty years.

"It's got something to do with the curve of the Cape," Mary explained to me. "That, and the Gulf Stream current."

"That's right," Maurice said. "The curve of the Cape."

"It makes some sort of an eddy out there in the ocean," Mary went on. "The storms get steered back out to sea."

"That's right, that's right," Maurice agreed. "Every time. Back out to sea."

On August 13, 2004, two months after we moved into the house, a smallish Category 2 storm, Hurricane Charley, spun off the northern coast of Cuba and curled through the warm bathwaters of the Gulf of Mexico, where it mutated, inexplicably, into a major Category 4 storm, and began registering sustained winds of 150 miles per hour. Evacuation orders were hastily issued for Tampa and most of the Gulf Coast, but Charley's rapid intensification and sudden turn caught everyone off-guard. The hurricane made landfall at 3:45 p.m., just west of Ft. Myers, near Cayo Costa.

The initial storm surge blew out a 450-meter-wide inlet through North Captiva Island (later named Charley's Cut), flooded Port Charlotte under 14 feet of water, scattered boats all over Punta Gorda, and generally turned the Gulf Coast into a missile strike zone. Charley was the most destructive Florida hurricane since Andrew, killing nine people and inflicting $17 billion worth of property damage. By evening, it had passed north of Cocoa Beach and left us with only the faintest, blithest breezes on the south side. Rather than serve as a wake-up call, Charley only seemed to reaffirm Mary and Maurice's belief in our invincibility.

But the wake-up call was coming. Two weeks later, a tropical wave developed in the far eastern Atlantic, somewhere between Barbados and Cape Verde, a massive low-pressure system that would coalesce into Hurricane Frances. Even in its early stages, Frances was twice the size of Charley. It was a slow mover, trawling westward like a transatlantic ship, all the while expanding and gathering water. When it rolled north over the Antilles, it grew into a behemoth—700 miles from tip to tip, wider and taller than the entire state of Florida.

We waited for the inevitable turn, but Frances kept driving west. On September 1, as the storm bore down on the Bahamas, Florida's governor, Jeb Bush, declared a state of emergency. Kennedy Space Center was shuttered up. The updated forecast predicted the eyewall to slam into Vero Beach, 50 miles south of us. Cape Canaveral remained at the uppermost portion of "the cone of probability." With every new forecast, the fated bend out to sea became more unlikely. The satellite image seemed to take up the whole of the Atlantic. Frances's eyewall alone was 80 miles wide, and a Vero Beach strike would put Brevard County on the dirty side, fielding the most violent winds and rain.

On September 2, with Frances still west of the Bahamas, an eerie wind began to blow in from the east. Not a sea breeze, exactly. Something foreign, unstable, a sirocco of Saharan dust, a lacework of electromagnetic particles. Mary was watering her gardenias on the front porch. Maurice was fiddling with some tools in the garage. A couple of the newer houses across the street were putting plywood up over their windows. We decided to take our bikes out and scope the rest of the town. Plywood was going up everywhere. People had spray-painted messages on the wood, alongside rough-sketched hurricane glyphs: "Frances stay away!" "Hunker down!"

We ran into one of the Eleventh Street crew, a musician by the name of Dave Miller, smoking a joint and coasting shirtless on his bike, the wind flicking his hair all over his face. "Better get ready," he said. "Shit's about to go down."

In the lead-up to a hurricane, all the seabirds vanish from the beach. Scythe-winged frigate birds appear above the coast, tacking high on a lonely airstream, their beaks pointed longingly to sea. The dogs go skittish and strain their leashes. Everyone you meet has compassionate eyes. They ask if you are staying or going. If you need any help.

Brittany and I decided to make a Home Depot run. We waited two hours in line for twelve sheets of plywood. The skies were still clear and blue, but strange smells were riding in on the east winds. We cut and hefted the plywood, drilled and screwed Tapcons into our fresh paint job.

Later that afternoon, we walked to the beach. Massive waves were pummeling the outer sandbars, whitewater rampaging a mile or more out to sea. The white noise and floating vapor gave everything the feel of a Fellini movie. Our voices sounded like other people's voices. Somewhere out of sight, a little girl shouted "Daddy!" The air had that same muffled, anticipatory susurration as in the instant just before a car crash.

The county ordered an evacuation of the barrier island that afternoon, and we watched Mary and Maurice load a couple of flower-print suitcases into the trunk of their Oldsmobile Cutlass. They tossed their hands up in abdication and drove off. They didn't bother to board up.

Around dusk, a deep-purple bruise welled up in the east, and the first rain bands came whipping in sideways bursts off the sea. I put on a parka and took a last walk around the house. The crowns of the cabbage palms were thrown back like Cherokee headdresses. The street signs wobbled. The electric lines sizzled.

The police rolled through before dark, chirping their sirens and announcing over bullhorns: "This is a mandatory evacuation. There will be no emergency services on the island. Now is your last chance to get out!"

We had our own logic for riding out the storm. I figured the house's two-by-twelve rafters would hold up in Category 3 winds. The possibility of tornadoes was a bit worrisome, but we trusted the block walls. We stowed our life vests and surfboards in the living room, just in case.

Sometime in the night, the front deadbolt began to rattle. The double doors were in-swinging and could conceivably blow open, so I pried off the casing and screwed a two-by-four brace across them, effectively sealing us inside.

The windows whistled and thumped. Pulses of rain battered our concrete flanks. We couldn't get to sleep, so we popped a bottle of Bordeaux and drank it on the couch while we tracked the storm. The eyewall was still spinning *east* of the Bahamas. Amazingly, these squalls were just the thin, outer tendrils of the storm.

Around midnight, the winds notched up again. The roof began to throb. A sudden explosion of lightning seemed to strike the roof, and with a chilling, high-pitched twang—like a violin string snapping—our power was gone. We crouched in the dark, listening with horror to the groan of the rafters and pule of the plywood.

The rain blasted the eastern walls like a fireman's hose, smacking and smacking for hours. The sliding door tracks flooded and water began to pour over the new wood floors. I tried to soak it up with towels, squeezing it out in buckets, but it seeped underneath the floorboards and bubbled up from the seams.

Within a few hours, the whole house was wet and musty. Odors of past inhabitants swelled out of the walls. Without power and with the windows boarded up, the blackness was complete. Outside, an ominous screech railed over the din of the storm, as if some giant piece of metal were being dragged over concrete.

The noises went on all that day, all that night, all the next day. The roof breathed and breathed. The rain doubled its barrage on the eastern walls. An inch of water rippled over the floors. We took turns napping, though neither of us could sleep for more than an hour at a time.

On the morning of September 3, after what seemed an eternity, a more sporadic rain started to spit against the southern wall. The winds were blowing more out of the south, which meant Frances had moved finally to the northwest.

The front door had ceased shaking, so I took down the brace. An hour later, I turned the handle carefully and peeked outside. The front porch was covered in an inch of sand. My truck was still in the driveway, but it was all white, powder-coated, as if after a blizzard. We staggered outside to assess the damage.

The shingles had been torn from Mary and Maurice's roof. The gutters were gone. And the fences. A power pole had snapped in two and hung like a broken mast. Wires twisted and swayed like the torn rigging. The trees were all shredded, sandblasted. A sheet-metal roof had peeled like aluminum foil off one of the houses across the street.

The whole road was snowed over with fine white sand. We climbed over a hill where the crossover used to be to have a look at the beach. The dunes had tried to fold landward, but the oceanfront condos had impeded their natural flow. The sand had piled up to the third-floor balconies. Waves shushed against the seawalls, undermining the foundations. Dock lumber, palm trunks, tires, and ropes littered the surf zone. To the north, the Eighth Street church steeple had snapped in two, thrust itself through the gambrel, and lodged there, hilt-up, like Excalibur.

For fifty years, Cocoa Beach had been spared the wrath of the *zemi*. Now all its weak points were exposed. Every gas station had crumpled like origami constructs. Houses built during the lax building-code era of the '70s and '80s had chucked their roofs like mortarboards. Most of the trailer homes had gone sailing. Pieces of Cocoa Beach floated up and down the Banana River. Frances had been a mere Category 2 at impact, but it was massive, and punishingly slow. After passing over the Bahamas, it had lurched into the lukewarm Gulf Stream and stalled out, consolidating its forces, as if considering what to do next. By the time the eyewall made landfall near Hutchinson Island, about 60 miles south of Cocoa Beach, we'd endured three days of increasingly violent rain and winds, this time from the wrong side, the north quadrant.

Now the intrepid locals who had ridden out the storm crept out from their hiding spots to pick through the rubble and cast aside branches. The bridges to the barrier island were all closed, and it would be a couple of days before emergency crews would come to secure the power lines and allow anyone else back on the island.

Frances was supposedly a fifty-year storm, a once-in-a-generation event. But the *zemi* wasn't finished. Before Florida Power & Light could restore our power, another hurricane, Jeanne, developed in the Atlantic and set itself on the exact same path. Again, we dragged the moist sheets of plywood out of the garage. Again, screwed them over the windows. Again, the island was evacuated, and again, the cops trolled through with their bullhorns.

Again, we hunkered down, rode it out.

Hurricane Jeanne, a Category 3 storm, drove into Florida's eastern flank on September 26, making landfall in nearly the exact same spot as Frances.

They run into each other in my mind, Frances and Jeanne. Recurring nightmares. The fire hose at the eastern walls. The tragic sloshing of the floors. The wailing of the world.

We went powerless for six weeks, powerless in a stifling, stagnant late-summer heat wave. We slept on waterlogged floors (since the ground was cooler than the bed) and subsisted on dry food or takeout from the lone downtown café running off generators.

All told, three hurricanes tore through Cocoa Beach in the span of two months. It was our first year in our first house, our first year as husband and wife. For someone who believes in neither coincidence nor providence, it was a difficult string of events to reconcile.

Hurricanes have a way of reminding us—especially those of us who live on the barrier island—that we inhabit delicate terrain, and that the things we assume to be solid are not necessarily so.

But the day after Jeanne passed, a clean, fresh wind blew out of the west. The bridges were still blockaded, no mainlanders could cross, but the locals who'd stayed climbed over little snowed-in one-story houses to check the ocean. And lo! The sea had become a most magnificent shade of blue. Out there, past the wrack and wreckage, shoulder-high walls of the purest glass were sleeking over a newly formed sandbar.

We surfed out back that day, Brittany and I, and a handful of the Eleventh Street crew. My memories of this blissed-out session—the tingle of the sun on my skin, Brittany soaring across a long diamond-studded right, the flawless west wind, the return of the seabirds—remain brighter and more vivid than all the rest of the trials of that windy season.

Why We Surf

~~~~~~~~~~~~~~~~~~~~~~~~~~~

We surf because we love the feeling of motion, the push and pull of the sea, the breathless drop, the round lean of a bottom turn, the glide of the high line, the transcendental, weightless discharge of the barrel. Because to fly, gull-like, and soar through section after section as the sky unfolds and the universe courses through our bodies, is to fuse with the boundless cosmos.

When we surf, we are simultaneously weightless and deeply rooted. We are literally *pouring* forward, a sensation that cannot be replicated on dry land.

We surf to inhabit that borderland between states of matter, that evanescent fringe between water and air.

We surf to balance our spiritual energies. When the sea goes flat for weeks on end, or we are locked inland, we find ourselves growing weaker, and we search for unnatural diversions. But when the waves return, we walk with a thin cushion of air beneath our feet, wholly disassociated from the worries of the world. No one is quite so blissed-out as a surfer after a three-hour session in clean, peeling waves.

We surf to remind ourselves that the only thing constant in this world is change. That every ride is temporary.

We surf to interrupt the flow of gravity. To detach our bodies from land. For a few escapist hours, we are no longer earthbound human beings. We are sea ghosts, wind spirits.

Like yoga or the martial arts, riding a wave—paddling, duck-diving, even the simple act of sitting on your board without tipping over—requires stability and symmetry, and becomes more natural with time and training. In surfing, as in the martial arts, we strive to attain equilibrium, unconsciousness of form, artistry of physical motion.

We surf to hear the music of the sea, infinitely more soothing than the honking, hurrying drone of the land.

We surf because if we didn't, we would dry out and die.

We surf because, like the Florida swells, we are only here for a short, slippery moment.

Slater, in Bronze

On November 17, 2010, the moment they pulled the tarp to reveal the Kelly Slater statue, State Road A1A swelled up and tilted ever-so-slightly seaward. City engineers working traffic for the ceremony confirmed the half-inch inclination of the road but could not explain why or how it happened. They could only speculate . . . Kelly Slater, after all, has transformed things far greater than roads.

Slater, the man who revolutionized a millennia-old sport, attended the unveiling. Triangle Park (a small, pedestrian-inaccessible cleft of landscaping where the road splits in two) was packed with adoring fans who stood behind hedges or up on ladders, eager to snap photographs of the living legend. Chairs were arranged on the grass for Kelly's family, his boyhood surfing crew, the mayor, and surfing icons like Matt Kechele and Dick Catri. Laudatory speeches were made. The governor provided a handwritten statement. When the strings were finally pulled for the great reveal, the congregation drew in a collective breath. Kelly walked a full circle around the sculpture, eyes glowing. The equilibrium of the barrier island teetered.

People lingered late, chattering excitedly, waiting their turn for a picture with the champ. By evening, the crowd disbanded. The statue remained. It's what statues do best. They're persistent that way. They remain, long after those who raised them are boxed away.

Drive down A1A from the north, and the sculpture will leap out at you and catch you by surprise. There it is—behind three tall flagpoles, partially obscured by cabbage palms, shop fronts, power lines—a masterfully wrought bronze figure. The fact that you are passing it at 44 miles per hour adds to the effect: a golden surfer appears out of nowhere and tail-slides across your line of sight. Its placement is symbolic. It marks the official entry into "the Streets" of Slater's fabled childhood.

The statue doesn't scream for your attention. He doesn't raise his sword to the heavens. He's not standing in a tall, grandiose pose, or even looking at you. He's crouched in a kick slide, one arm cocked over his head, the other thrust forward, daggerlike, at a parallel angle to the surfboard.

Then he is behind you. And the elegant gesture has been imprinted on your mind.

Approach the Kelly Slater statue by foot (the most accessible parking spots are at the gas station immediately south of the triangle), and the first thing you will notice is the graceful handling of the upper hand. There, in the detail of Slater's fingers, is the hyperrealism of Greek sculpture... supple, fluid of wrist, a magician's hand, simultaneously beckoning the ocean and withdrawing from it.

The sculptor, Tasha Drazich, rendered the pose from a 1998 Tom Dugan photo taken at Sebastian Inlet, in which Slater is executing a "tomahawk chop" cutback high on the wave face, and throwing off a prodigious fan of spray.[1] Drazich met the challenge of capturing the maneuver in bronze through the inventive use of a live model suspended on ropes.

The leaning aspect of the piece calls to mind Frederic Remington's 1857 bronze *Mountain Man,* in which a horse and rider are caught in the act of descending a precipitous slope. Like Remington's sculpture, the bronze Slater's ankles are fixed, his weight shifted to the back. And yet Slater is more controlled than the Mountain Man, his motion down the line more decisive.

If you stand at the base of the statue, you cannot help but notice the giant toes . . . bearish, overlarge, with the element of Rodin in the pressed flesh. Peer closer and observe another curiosity: every inch of Slater's skin is striated with tiny lines, as if the bronze has been run over with a surfer's wax comb.

Now, an upward glance at the face. You are struck with the feeling that this is not quite Kelly's face . . . Something is off. Is it the nose? The eyes? The irisless orbs emit a sort of transcendent distance. The original photograph depicted a younger Kelly, head full of hair, neck taut with

1 From the pages of *Eastern Surf Magazine* (words by Dick "Mez" Meseroll): "Dugan's award winning snap of Kelly from the 'Honey Hole' angle next to the Sebastian Inlet jetty went on to be on Australia Surfing Life's 'Best 50 Photos Of All Time' . . . the huge, sheeting, crystal fan of water displacement, the puffed up fish lips as Kelly exhales through the turn and the sublime form including placement of his arms and perfect body mechanics as he torques through this massive, railed out arc on his brother Sean's board. In a word, mesmerizing."

Kelly Slater's iconic "tomahawk chop," Sebastian Inlet, 1991.

Photograph by Tom Dugan.

The bronze Kelly Slater statue at Third Street North, marking the entry to "the Streets" of Slater's fabled childhood.

Photograph by Tom Dugan.

exertion. Here we have the iconic later-era shaved head Slater, and this strange, serene face, monk-like in its calmness.

The surfboard—shaped by Kechele—was the trickiest element of the statue to reproduce in the bronze forge. Its surface is smooth as a bell, the rails full and rounded. It has no fin, perhaps so that the untrained eye might not think Slater is surfing backward. The surfboard is mounted on a domed base, where nine of Slater's eleven world titles are engraved on the bronze (2010 and 2011 have yet to be added).

Walking, like Kelly, full circle around the statue, you can appreciate the cut of the shoulders, the muscles of the calves, the shape of the jaw-line. The physical gifts of the gymnast coupled with the creative inspiration of the artist. The aura is undeniable—this could be no one else but Kelly Slater. Here, in the extra layer of air beneath the board, in the supreme balance, is the steady and unflinching suggestion that through thought alone we guide ourselves through time and space.

The fact that the greatest surfer of all time first dipped a board into these very waters, these mushy waves of Cocoa Beach, is instructive for those who consider these sorts of things. Every time we drive past the Kelly Slater statue, it reminds us that treasure might be found in the least expected places.

A Field Guide to Spring Break, Cocoa Beach

Each spring, legions of colorful and exotic species descend upon the beaches of Central Florida to bathe in the warming waves, consume excessive quantities of beer, and commence their yearly mating rituals. This guide will help the naturalist identify various migratory species of Cocoa Beach and surrounding areas during the Spring Break season.

The Day-Tripper (Barbaro Orange Countius)

Easily the most abundant of all nonlocal species, the Day-Tripper is ubiquitous in the region throughout the year, but their population balloons during the month of March, consuming whole swaths of coastline. Their vehicles are conspicuous with their polished rims, heavy bass thrums, and flashy baubles dangling from rearview mirrors. Males are best viewed from afar, as they will exhibit aggressive behavior toward humans and automobiles while attempting to cross the road, especially while in heat. Females are typically ornamented with tattoos on the lower backs, or (in the more dangerous varietals) on the necks or behind the ears. Males mark their territory by urinating on buildings or sidewalks and are distinguishable by their sneering lips and the trail of litter that accumulates in their wake. Owing to the proximity of their Orlando-area nests, Day-Trippers subsist on a scant diet of cheap beer and cigarettes while beachside. Natural habitat: Minutemen Causeway, The Pier.

The Disney Spillover (Familius Cluelessicae)

Disney Spillovers hail from as far north as Canada and as far west as Kansas. They typically travel en masse and are brightly plumed with decorative T-shirts, camera straps, umbrellas, and plastic Ron Jon bags. Be

Spring is migratory season in Cocoa Beach.

Illustration © John Klossner. www.jklossner.com

sure to observe slow speed zones at Spillover crossings, as they tend to be discombobulated, and their young attracted to fast-moving vehicles. Mothers usually carry their babies in one arm with the other hand extended behind them, as if seeking out another wayward child. Dazed, agitated, easily burned, the Spillover gravitates toward major intersections. Best viewing spot: corner of 520 Causeway and A1A.

The Snowbird (Retirus Traffictera)

The Snowbird hails from Ohio, Illinois, Michigan, Pennsylvania, and the Great Plains. A roaming species, they travel by RV, van, bicycle, or on foot. Distinctive features include a bluish tint to the head feathers, high, pressed shorts, Panama hats, and wire-rimmed glasses. They travel in pairs and are mostly harmless, except when behind the wheel of a car, when they become the deadliest of all migratory species. They are known to drive against traffic on one-way roads, make slow, sweeping right turns from left lanes, and stick their tails perilously out from medians.

The Kook (Flailos Kookaburra)

The Common Kook bears some resemblance to the local surfer but is easily recognized by his Volcom stickers, the surfboards strapped backward or sideways to his car, and the beer cooler rolling behind him as he roams the beach. Unlike the local fauna, the Kook will regularly despoil the dune ecosystem, leave waste in parking lots, and give the "stink eye" to other surfers. Another feature is a milky coloration to the skin. Kooks are generally drawn to the more crowded breaks. When there are waves, Kooks can be seen sitting on crossovers in their neon-green tank tops or struggling in the breakwaters on a pop-out board far too small for their skill level.

The German Tourist (Eccentricus Deutchlandia)

Renowned for their tall, lithe figures, Speedos, swimming goggles, and reflective white skin (which protects them by blinding potential predators), German Tourists speak in high, garbled voices and perform a distinctively bizarre swimming ritual, in which they warm up by flapping the arms and touching the toes, and then proceed to drown themselves in the shorepound.

The New Jerseyite (Snookius Spraytanua)

More widespread in Pensacola and Daytona Beach, stray groups of New Jerseyites can sometimes drift as far south as Cocoa Beach. The male's head is uncommonly spiked and gelled, even at the back of the skull. After consuming a twelve-pack, his chest will puff out, and he will put on a preening spectacle, loudly barking while repeatedly sliding his hands through his hair. Females are expressive, habitually pugnacious, and are usually considered more dangerous than the males. Best viewing time is early in the day, when New Jerseyites are at their most tranquil. At sunset, they will move inland from the coast, seeking out the revelry and mating havens of the Inner Room Cabaret or Cheater's Adult Entertainment Lounge.

The Hobo Salt (Griftae Spareaquarterum)

The migratory Hobo Salt is virtually indistinguishable from the local breed—both are characterized by a reddish tint, lack of teeth, heavy beards, and long, matted hair. The Salt will curl up if threatened, and presents no danger to the casual onlooker. He is the only species not to shed its heavy coat in the warmth of spring. Habitat: the Salt exists at the fringes of major Spring Break hubs and can also be found enjoying free coffee at the local Publix.

The Hot Mess (Drunkus Bikinae)

The Hot Mess appears only in the evening, stumbling along back alleys or flopping repeatedly onto sidewalks. She is a rare, solitary bird usually spotted in random stages of undress. Her mating call varies but might resemble the caterwaul of a coyote. Tattoos typically stripe the lower back or ankles. Approaching a Hot Mess is inadvisable, as her presence can attract hordes of mating Day-Trippers, Kooks, and Frat Boys. Proximity can lead to serious injury or even death.

The Brooklyner (J. Lovium Bootilicious)

Brooklyners travel in familial flocks. Males are recognizable by their glistening faux diamond studs, silver neck chains, sneakers, and white socks pulled up to midcalf. Females are often robust and energetic, with a rhythmic mating dance typified by raised elbows, outthrust rear, and legs bent out wide. They are for the most part amiable creatures and tend to keep in tight packs, with the males engrossed in their smartphones.

The Frat Boy/Sorority Girl (Frattus Juvenalium)

A distant relative of the Day-Tripper, this species differentiates itself from the Barbaro Orange Countius in its more muscular physique, attentive grooming habits (the males often have shaved chests), and paucity of tattoos. They travel with a bevy of coolers, footballs, boom boxes, and beach chairs. While lively and courteous in the morning, after heavy alcohol consumption the males transform into the most malignant of all beach species. Warning signs of such a metamorphosis include a dulling of the eye sockets and a loose swagger, accompanied by a hanging of the hands.

The Lurker (Sketchus Pervops)

Wiry, with a shuffling gait, tattooed neck, long jean shorts, and a wedge-shaped head, the lurker is a peculiar creature whose habits are mostly unknown. He has never been seen without a cigarette in his mouth or behind one ear. His sneakers are suspiciously new and white. It is advisable to keep a safe distance. Lurkers are known to perch on the dune crossovers for hours at a time, casting malicious glances at children and parked cars.

The Adventurer (Visitorium Respectus)

The most uncommon bird of all, the Adventurer will do its best to blend in with the laid-back, friendly atmosphere of the seaside town. This camouflaging technique allows it to enjoy Spring Break at the proper speed, free of distress or misfortune. Habitat varies but might be seen paddleboarding on the river, lounging at the most serene beaches, or sipping coffee at local haunts like the Surfinista Café.

Dick Catri, 1938–2017

〜〜〜〜〜〜〜〜〜〜

When a revered member of the surf community dies, surfers hold a
paddle-out ceremony to honor their life and commit their spirit into sea.
This write-up for Dick Catri's memorial service originally appeared in
Surfer magazine.

On Saturday, June 10, 2017, after a week of ruthless floods and thunderstorms, Sebastian Inlet awoke to a blue and windless sky. The cars came
pouring down the bridge and overfilled the parking lot. Hundreds of pilgrims gathered on the south side of the jetty to honor the life of Florida's
original surf legend, the chieftain of this barrier island: Dick Catri.

Catri—the first Florida boy to charge Pipeline and Waimea, first to
deliver Hawaii savvy to the East Coast, first to coach phenomena like
Gary Propper and Kelly Slater—asked that his ashes be cast into Monster Hole, a sharky, deepwater mysto left that breaks a quarter mile past
the jetty, and where, sixty years ago, during a massive storm swell, Catri
and Jack "Murf the Surf" Murphy were the first to paddle out and ride
the waves over the outer sandbar.

"This was a shark channel," Murphy told me. "Loaded with 13-foot
hammerheads and leopard sharks." Murphy—robust and upright,
eighty years old, aristocratic, infamous for jewel heists and murder—
raised an eyebrow at the Atlantic. "But we had a deal with the sharks.
They stayed under the water and we stayed on top."

One by one, surfers stood up to hallow their captain. They painted
the young Catri as a wild man, driving bare-ass naked across Texas in a
'57 Chevrolet, charging Pipe with Jock Sutherland and Butch Van Artsdalen, dropping in on Sunset bombs in the Duke Invitational. But the
tales of his Florida exploits stirred the pilgrims the most. Mimi Munro,
the youngest member of Catri's '67 Hobie team, described him as a brilliant coach, an innovative promoter, and a father figure to a group of

Dick Catri (*left*), charging Waimea on a longboard, no leash, early '60s.
Photograph courtesy of the Florida Surf Museum.

young, budding surf stars—including Propper, Mike Tabeling, Fletcher Sharpe, Sam Gornto, and Bruce Valluzzi—who went on to become the winningest surf team in history.

The day got steamy, sweaty, spiritual. The tide was dropping, and waves began to break in earnest on the outside. Hundreds of surfboards lay on the grass, many of them shaped by Catri himself, or originally sold out of one of his shops, Primo's or Shagg's. They were mementos to his legacy: Nuuhiwa models, experimental '70s boards, pintails, twin-fins, thrusters. Rock star shapers like Ricky Carroll got up to profess their undying debt to the Captain, conjured a Catri covered in foam dust, shaping alongside the likes of Jim Phillips, Johnny Rice, and Greg Loehr.

Clouds piled up on the western horizon. Some of the younger generation stood on the sidelines and expounded on the older, bearded Catri. "He taught us how to barrel-ride, how to handle heavy current," said Todd Holland, a Catri disciple turned Pipe charger. "We surfed the high tide shorepound at Indialantic, and he got us prepared for faster, more powerful waves. He built me my first Hawaii board, a 5'9" balsa twin-fin."

The clouds rolled up over the bridge, casting cool shadows on the ceremony, softening the heat of the day. The Florida surfers, who know better than to take any surfing conditions for granted, picked up their boards and ventured out past the wrack line.

This pristine stretch of beach, this place called Sebastian Inlet, training ground of champions, will forever belong to Dick Catri, who fought for the right of surfers on First Peak, who once threw a fisherman off the jetty for lobbing a sinker through the nose of his board, and who came to be called the Godfather of East Coast surfing.

The pilgrims scattered their flowers into the sea. Set waves came rolling up from the outside and sent whitewater fizzling through the inner circle. When Dick Catri's ashes dissolved into the blue, moving waters, the surfers paddled to the outside, hoping to catch one last ride with the Captain at Monster Hole.

Holding the Line

To the people of Cocoa Beach, the 2004 hurricane season had all the makings of biblical allegory: unrelenting rains, rising floodwaters, the eschatological vision of a wall of sand heaving skyward and enveloping their town. In the aftermath of Frances and Jeanne, locals who had lived in a mostly undisturbed trance on this seaside enclave for fifty years were forced to question their most fundamental assumptions of peace and safety.

They shoveled sand off their front porches, scavenged through the grist and rubble. The more devout among them glanced skyward and remembered that old parable about the wise man, who built his house on the rock, and the foolish one, who built his on the sand. *The rain descended, the floods came, and the winds blew and beat upon their house.* As they recalled, things had not gone too well for the fool.

Bobcats and backhoes scraped sand off the eastern walls. Loaders growled up and down A1A, embanking white berms along both sides of the road. Fleets of beaconed boom trucks from Alabama and Louisiana rolled in to assist FPL, the local power company. Teams in neon vests worried with the overhead whips, erected new light poles and transformers. Many of the pre-wind-code houses of the '70s were demolished; others were stripped to their concrete bones. The gas stations were leveled. Blue tarps rippled over the rooflines.

Concerned citizens gathered at city council meetings to discuss what soon presented as the most pressing problem—the erosion of the beaches. The sand was gone, and waves were lapping at people's backyards. Houses teetered precariously over the high-tide line. The properties on the east side of A1A stood at the crest of the dune system, the highest topographical elevation on the island. If the shoreline were breached, there would be nothing left for the sea to do but flow downhill and flood the rest of the town.

They called in engineers and planners, pocket-protector types who kept referring to the "avulsion" of the sand. Some warned that higher sea temperatures could very well lead to more frequent hurricanes, with greater chances for rapid intensification. A new concept was beginning to creep into the minds of the people of Cocoa Beach—this idea that the ground beneath their feet was evanescent and unreliable. The scientists' subtext was sinister enough: it was quite possible that 2004 was not an outlier season at all but a harbinger of things to come.

To do nothing was out of the question. To do nothing was to watch the next storm surge cascade over A1A. But solutions would not come cheaply, or easily. The fastest and most cost-effective fix was to simply "renourish" the beach, that is, to replace the missing sand by pumping it in from somewhere else. Here was the basic twenty-first-century coastal reinforcement tenet: imported sand creates a buffer zone, a sacrificial killing field where storm surge impacts can be dampened and mitigated. Build the beaches back up so the sand absorbs the brunt of the wave energy before the houses do.

Back in 1999, a group of Brevard County attorneys had won a lawsuit against the Army Corps of Engineers that found the federal government liable for interrupting the natural north-south flow of sand with the construction of the Port Canaveral inlet and jetties in 1954. The lawyers were able to prove that the jetty blockage had been effecting long-term erosion to Cocoa Beach. The judge ordered the Army Corps to cover the expense of replacing the lost sand for the next fifty years—until 2049. Thus, in the spring of 2005, the people of Cocoa Beach were able to round up $29 million federal dollars to hire a dredging company, set up a temporary pipeline, pump sand out of the Canaveral Shoals, and dump it directly into their littoral zone.

Surfers are the sentinels of the beach, so it follows that they were some of the most vocal opponents of the dredge. Surfers were the first to sight the 200-yard-long hopper dredges on the horizon, and to walk past the giant rusty pipes laid north-to-south above the high-tide line. Their beach accesses were shut down, cordoned off. They watched as the hopper dredges—floating goliaths, property of Weeks Marine, a contractor from the Great Lakes—discharged shoal-sand slurry at a rate of 1,000 cubic meters per hour into iron-caged boxes on the shore, where dozers awaited the explosive discharge and rough-graded the newly formed beach. The ocean, stirred and agitated, turned gray-brown and silty. The beaches reeked of dead mollusks. The surfers who did venture past the ropes for an illicit session had to shush through gray, ragged shoal sands, their feet sinking to the ankles. They cursed the dredge material and began referring to it as "ashtray sand."

Kelly Slater, Cocoa Beach's illustrious son, had this take on the sand dredging: "They came and they decided to take sand from a quarter mile off the beach and dump it on the beach. It's a completely different sand. It goes through a whole life cycle of changing its consistency. We used to have that real powdery sand, white sand, that squeaks up on the beach. It's rare to find that now. Now we've got this gray sand, full of shells. The natural flow of the sand has changed completely."

John Hearin, a local waterman and the chairman of the Cocoa Beach branch of the Surfrider Foundation, was so concerned with the type of sand coming out of the Canaveral borrow site that he penned his doctoral dissertation on it: "A Detailed Analysis of Beach Nourishment and Its Impact on the Surfing Wave Environment of Brevard County, Florida." Hearin noted that the Florida Department of Environmental Protection standards require imported sand to "maintain the general character of the beach, including grain size, color, and mineral composition." His analysis of the new sand found Slater's observations to be spot-on—the fill sediment from the Canaveral Shoals II borrow site consisted of larger and coarser grains than the native sand. This mismatched material transformed Cocoa Beach's sea floor from a "dissipative" surf zone, which breaks at all tides, to an "intermediate-reflective" one, or a tidal-dependent beach with more closeouts. "At higher tides," Hearin wrote, "the waves would plunge much closer to shore (as shore pound) and in some cases, shut down altogether."

In the short term, the 2005 dredging would add 60 feet of sand to Cocoa Beach's dune system, but it was a pyrrhic victory for the locals, especially the surfers. Since the sand was less compact, it was easier to draw out, and subsequent swells took bites out of the beach. The gray matter washed out to sea. Scarps formed, head-high bluffs dropping down from the high tide line to the water. Deep troughs developed 20 yards from shore, creating rip currents, hazardous swimming conditions, and effectively ruining the nearshore profile for years to come.

The fleeting benefits of the sand dredging raised existential questions, not to mention political ones. How long would taxpayers be able to subsidize the replacement of such fragile foundations? Would pumping and dumping be enough to fend off the big one, the storm that wrapped the sea into the river and cracked up the town? Likely not. Long-term municipal planning would be needed to mitigate that risk, costly structural improvements like raising the infrastructure of the island in place, building jetties, or contriving a permanent sand bypass system around the port.

Sand is a valuable component in a comprehensive shoreline protection strategy. Alone, it is as ephemeral as wind.

Cocoa Beach's addiction to imported dredge sand, in the end, might not be sustainable. There is no escaping the fact that, soon enough, the ocean will breach the island. Not in one place, but in many. At some point, the rising seas will be too relentless. Future generations will endure repeated storm surges and flooding. If the people of Cocoa Beach don't plan responsibly, if they don't map out long-term strategies for the future, their last resort will be to move inland and seek higher ground.

A beach is a wash zone, after all. Sand is just a trillion crushed and tumbled bits of shell, bone, and shattered castles. One day, a flood tide will wash away these houses built on the sand. For now, the beachside residents buy themselves another season.

The Birth of Style

We spent the fall after the storms reinforcing the bulwarks: ripping out the water-damaged baseboards, installing accordion shutters, replacing the French doors with impact-glass sliders, and calling in a roofer to replace the beat-up three-tab roof with architectural shingles. On those crisp, sunny days after a cold front passed through, we'd open the windows and let the dry breeze blow through the house. The oak floors—which had buckled from the flooding—began to relax and lay down (in time, we would grow to love them for all their ridges and imperfections).

Winter came, and with it the north swells. Brittany was finishing up her last year of university in Orlando, and I was still driving back and forth to construction sites in Tampa, but with some luck and proper planning we were able to carve out days for likely surf sessions. This was before the dredge, and we surfed Eleventh Street, our home break. We were learning to balance our obligations with surfing, to judge success not by money or status but by how much time we spent out in the water.

To maintain a steady surfing routine in Florida—where short-lived, wind-dependent swells punctuate weeklong stretches of flat, lake-like conditions—is to hitch yourself onto a manic, alternating regimen of Zen-like patience and split-second readiness. Surfing here requires a compulsive willingness to drop everything the moment the wind turns and a readiness to accept the possibility of getting skunked—of driving around for an hour without finding anything to ride and going home without getting wet.

I was lucky to have in Brittany a willing co-conspirator, someone who understood the particular delusions that fueled a Florida surfer's days. When your wife surfs, you have a permanent hall pass. If the swell and wind are cooperating, the world can wait. Woe to the surfer with the landlocked spouse!

In spring we worked like garden imps in the backyard, planting Green Island ficus, queen palms, and plumeria trees with two-toned pink lemonade flowers that smelled of citrus and vanilla. We were young and optimistic, and every leaf and blade of grass seemed impossibly lovely and meaningful. When we weren't surfing or landscaping, we were coasting through town on our bicycles. If we rode at just the right speed, with the winds at our backs, yellow paper-thin butterflies would flicker about our heads like fairies.

No hurricanes threatened the barrier island all that next season. But it was 2005, the year of Katrina, and we watched on the news as the Category 5 storm pummeled New Orleans, ruptured the levees, flooded the Ninth Ward, knocked out power across Louisiana, erased 500 square miles of coastal wetlands, and killed more than one thousand people. As if we needed another reminder of the vulnerability of all water-facing peoples.

Before the sand dredging, the waves at Eleventh Street were long, smooth, playful beach breaks. Most days we could scrounge up something to ride. But after the "renourishment," even on perfect 3–4-foot swells, the waves would wall up, blue and beautiful as before, then struggle through the trough like deepwater swells, incapable of releasing their energy, wobble to the inside, and crash in heartbreaking closeouts on the beach. High tide or low, surfing at our home break had become a hopeless proposition. We were forced to load the surfboards into the bed of the pickup truck and hunt out other sandbars.

The first spot to come back to life after the dredge was the Cocoa Beach Pier. The pilings extended 800 feet out to sea, partially blocking the north-south drift of nearshore sand and building up a sand salient, a zone of shallower water where waves would pitch up on the outside and feather evenly toward shore. North winds often accompanied the winter swells, and the south side, in the lee of the structure, was calmer and glassier. The rip current that flowed out to sea next to the pier allowed you to hug the pilings and enjoy a dry-hair slide out to the lineup.

The pier had been a crowded surf spot even before the dredge. Now that everywhere else from Cocoa Beach down to Melbourne Beach had shut down, the pier surf zone became overrun with all manner of surfers—kooks, shredders, longboarders, boogie boarders—all jockeying for position. Drop-ins, board-cracking collisions, and dustups were all too common.

Surfing in the pack demanded a heightened awareness and respect. Brittany and I learned to hang on the shoulder, watch the sets come through, and assess the talent in the water—specifically those we should defer to when paddling for a wave—before trying to establish ourselves in the lineup.

It was edifying, spending time out in the water with the area's top surfers. We studied their style and mimetically, subconsciously incorporated it into our own. How they took off behind the peak of the wave, or remained prone for that extra second before popping up into the speed section. We cultivated the mannerisms of those ultratalented, million-wave Florida surfers . . . always ripping, always desperate for more, and always so blasé about the whole thing.

Of the regulars at the pier, no one was more influential or inspirational to us than James MacLaren. In his youth, he'd been a legendary rabble-rouser who'd haunted the north shore of Hawaii, camped out for years in an old concrete bunker, surfed Sunset with the likes of Jock Sutherland, and returned to Cocoa Beach in the '70s to work at NASA, write books on surfing, and regulate lineups up and down the Florida coast. Now he was a sixty-something-year-old Zen master, a holy lunatic, and a noseriding wizard. At the pier, MacLaren would sit on the far outside—his grey curls shining, a giant-headed satyr—and pick off the biggest set waves, brazenly commandeering his 10'4" Claude Codgen-shaped longboard through the melee of bobbing heads, cross-stepping to the tip and flying through section after impossible section, riding switchfoot, backward, wielding his hands like a mad orchestral composer.

In his manic, high-pitched voice, MacLaren would shout out praises or rebukes: "We love it when a beautiful girl cross steps with brio and dash!" or, to some VAL in his way, "Paddle down the beach, fuckwad! You are now officially *persona non grata!*" When he wasn't surfing, MacLaren would stalk the beach with his Nikon, snapping photographs for his local surf report website, which he would post alongside captions that read like poetic screeds or aesthetic treatises. MacLaren was especially partial to the girls; he hosted female-friendly Socratic sessions at the library, in which he would analyze their surfing pictures and offer insight into positioning, rail control, or noseriding modalities.

Through MacLaren we learned the proper technique for waxing our surfboards (in small circles, flat of the wax to the board, skimming your fingernails on the surface as you buff), how to read the tide by observing the moon's height in the sky (counterintuitively, low tide corresponds to the moon at its zenith), or the changing face of the water (the texture and color of the surface augur its depths), and why surfing without a leash is crucial for every noseriding aspirant (the cord restricts your freedom to walk; you can only foster true synergy with your board if you don't abandon it at the end of your ride).

The devotional act of slipping over the surface of the sea was changing us, spiritually and physically. Prolonged exposure to the ionized spindrift was reconfiguring our mitochondria. Our hair grew lighter, longer, our skin browner, our muscles looser. I was thirty, Brittany twenty-five. We were breaking out of our cocoon of kookdom, emerging as surfers.

We sought out more remote spots, secret mini-shoals that for weeks at a time would light up, unnoticed by the maddening crowds. A left might be purring off some secret sandbar at Sixth Street while Fifth and Seventh remained flat as a lake. We drove around, found the mysto break—at the Driftwood House, a beach shack built out of shipwreck cypress in 1912, or at Hangars, where the submerged pilings of the old Patrick Pier were suddenly resurrecting the waves of old. We attempted new maneuvers, took deeper lines, refined our stances, pushed our noseriding to the next level.

If we lived by one principal philosophy, it was this: to maximize our moments of beauty. By doing so, by encouraging the world to shimmer and sing, we believed we could actually slow down time itself. And it worked . . . those first few halcyon years in Cocoa Beach were richer and more full of impressions than all of my first twenty-five.

Seek and you will find beauty in every pocket of sun and shadow. A rocket ship—a strip of fire in the north—lifting off in a pillar of alabaster smoke. A lone pelican coasts on high, dipping its wingtip, as if to acknowledge us as kindred spirits. Standing in the middle of the road one afternoon, dripping wet and awestruck, still breathing heavily from our last waves, we watch the western sky erupt in a three-dimensional filigree of pink light, a lattice of flame billowing up from the river.

Here is a vision that will remain with me until the very end: I'm sitting on the outside with Brittany, a glassy day, floating on a sea of gemstones, seagulls streaking on the lilac haze. A set approaches; Brittany straightens up, spins her board, paddles, and disappears behind the fulminating rise. The wind lifts her hair. Her hands rise as if in supplication. As she races down the line, the tail block of her board simmers and boils in the back of the wave like a fiery blade. The whole of the barrier island—the whole of the cosmos—bends behind her, rejoices.

Lucky. We were lucky. The 2006 hurricane season came and went, one of the quietest on record. That was the summer we conceived our daughter.

For nine months, Brittany had to keep her surfboard on the rack. Sometimes she would set up a chair and watch my session. Between sets, I'd admire the queenly vision of her sitting in the sun. But I missed her company out in the water and lamented all her missed waves. I promised her eternal priority[1] when she returned to the lineup—she could drop in on me anytime, anywhere, for the rest of her life.

In March 2007, Brittany gave birth to our daughter, our firstborn—Aubrey—at Cape Canaveral Hospital. She insisted on delivering under her own strength and refused the Pitocin and the epidural. She was a goddess. I've never admired anyone more. From our room on the sixth floor, we had a stunning view of the Banana River. The clouds were all pink and tangerine, like a riot of hibiscus flowers. The dolphins leapt in celebration. It was the first day of spring.

---

1   Priority (as defined by the World Surf League): "The surfer with priority has the unconditional right of way to catch any wave they choose. Other surfers in the heat can paddle for, and catch, the same wave, but only if they do not hinder the scoring potential of a surfer with priority . . . If two or more surfers catch a wave, the first surfer to make it to the take-off zone will get priority."

Three World Champions

The total populace of Brevard County's barrier island—from Kennedy Space Center down to Sebastian Inlet—numbers only 54,000 people. For such a sparsely inhabited community to produce three best-in-the-world athletes is a feat unmatched in the history of modern sports. Yet there it is: Kelly Slater, CJ Hobgood, and Caroline Marks all rode their first waves here, all grew up here, and all went on to win world surfing titles. To grasp the scope of such a coincidence, imagine if Roger Federer, Serena Williams, and Novak Djokovic all came up playing tennis on the same provincial courts of Tinley Park, Illinois (population 54,000).

Fact: a tenacious grom looking to be crowned world champion of the World Surf League has a better chance starting off here, on Florida's Space Coast, than anywhere else on Earth.

Just watch any random Cocoa Beach grom slashing dragonfly-inspired S-turns on a warm, overcast afternoon and you'll understand the depth of talent here. Drop any five Satellite Beach rippers into the lineup at any break in the world; you can be sure they will outclass the field.

But what is it about this place that makes the kids so special?

Plenty of other coastlines have warm climates, sandy beach breaks, easy access to the surf. Why do you think so many world champions hail from Brevard County?

Caroline Marks:[1] Obviously, Florida doesn't have the best waves. At all. We don't have much variety. The period doesn't get over four-

---

1   Caroline Marks: Born 2002. Goofyfoot. World Surf League Champion: 2023. Olympic Gold Medalist: 2024. Child prodigy out of Melbourne Beach. Unmatched backside power and speed off the bottom. Expressive, aggressive, improvisational. Relaxed and technically polished on the gnarliest waves in the world—Sunset Beach, Teahupo'o, Pipeline. Young, poised, valiant, she rides with the air of a Hawaiian chiefess.

Caroline Marks, making it look easy in a heavy place—slotted atTeahupo'o—on her way to winning the Olympic gold.

Photograph AP Photo/Gregory Bull.

teen seconds. We just have beach breaks. It's usually closed out. But we aren't jaded. I think there's a lot to be said about that. When we travel, we just have that froth and that drive to surf all day long, when the waves are good *and* when the waves are bad.

CJ Hobgood:[2] If you took a guy from the West Coast, let's say he's twenty years old. Ok, how many waves did he catch in his lifetime? I think we've gotten more reps. You could say the reps were not as long. An average ride on the West Coast might be seven seconds, and the average ride on the East Coast only four seconds. But we put way more time in. We whacked the golf ball. We hit the tennis ball. Whatever analogy you want to use. We hit it a lot more times.

---

2 CJ Hobgood: Born 1979. Goofyfoot. World Champion: 2001. Rocket-fueled aerialist, barrel-riding, double-hand-dragging sorcerer. Identical twin to Damien Hobgood, former world number seven. Teleportation-like ability to instantly materialize on any section on a wave. Instinctual, fearless, willing to throw himself over the ledge or stall into perilous pits. Hometown: Satellite Beach.

Kelly Slater:[3] In Florida, the crowds are limited, there's short interval, lots of waves; they're slow, but you have to be really precise. Because making a mistake on a small wave is much easier than making a mistake on a bigger wave. You have more room for error on a bigger wave. When it's slower, you gotta be really precise. There's something good about learning in slow motion but having to be tack-sharp with that. I think that translates out to going faster on bigger waves, a bigger canvas. There's a benefit in the overall number of rides you get, growing up where there are short-interval waves. Especially a beach break, because it's not breaking in just one spot, it breaks anywhere and you learn different angles, and you take notice of little rips, or the effect the previous wave had on the wave you're on. You're always looking for a little more pocket of energy or speed to refine what you're trying to do, and if those waves are moving slower—typically all the east coast waves are, whether you're east coast Australia, or even Hawaii, Japan, Brazil, all the east coasts on different continents tend to have the shorter-interval wave—it's easier to learn how to manhandle those waves to some degree.

What was life like as a kid here?

Caroline Marks: We had about an acre of land. I never was really on my phone much. I never really played video games. I was always outdoors. I have a really big family. I'm one of six. We were the gathering house; we'd have friends and extra people over all the time. We would either go to the river, fish all day, or surf all day. We had a little dirt bike track in our backyard, and a half pipe. Just a full playground for kids. We grew up outdoors and active, and I'd just hang out with my brothers all day. When I was nine I started to really get into surfing. I looked up to my older brothers, and they did it, they thought it was cool. I really wanted their approval and wanted them to think I was cool. I grew up having to have thick skin, with

---

3 Kelly Slater: Born 1972. Regularfoot. World Champion: 1992, 1994–98, 2005–6, 2008, 2010–11. Surfing's Muhammad Ali, Michael Jordan, Tom Brady. The undisputed GOAT. Unrivaled explosiveness, creativity, vision. Feet like suction cups. Winner of every contest known to man, including the Eddie Aikau Big Wave Invitational. Magician, perfectionist, catcher of last-minute chandeliers, dealer in unreality, legend from the time he was an eight-year-old prodigy to his mythological victory at Pipeline at the age of fifty. Hometown: Cocoa Beach.

my brothers. They're pretty gnarly. In the most loving way possible, they're pretty harsh on me. The way my whole family works, if you're going to do something, you're going to try your hardest to be the best at it. I'm really glad I had that.

Tell me about your first surfboard.

Kelly Slater: I rode Styrofoam boards we bought at the thrift store, molded Styrofoam with molded in fins, almost like a finless board like Derek Hynd[4] used to ride. I would actually stand up and surf on it. I graduated from that when I was six or so. I got this boogie board with two fins. We ordered it from a surf magazine. It had a leash I wore on my left wrist. It was super flexy. It worked because I was so small. It was thick. It didn't bend too much because I was so light. It actually was a twin-fin. So I could go down the line and turn on it. I won my first contest on that when I was eight. It was the Salick Brothers Contest, in 1980. Later that year I got my custom Salick board from them.

That was your local surf shop? The Salick Brothers?

Kelly Slater: Yeah, it was a block back from the beach, at the Islander Hut.[5] I'd ride my bike there. I remember the high-gloss new surfboards in the racks with really beautiful airbrushes. It seemed like each one was a special art piece.

What was your home break?

CJ Hobgood: It was Peg-leg's, Mark Realty, or SOBs [named after the restaurant Sun on the Beach]. Wherever you could ride your bike was the spot. And then when some of our older friends started driving, the inlet was the place to be. It was always going to be the best spot—Sebastian. There were always going to be the best surfers there, and there were always going to be some photogs there, so when someone wanted to drive you to Sebastian Inlet, you're in, and you're styling.

---

4 Derek Hynd: Australian surfer/author whose advocacy for "free friction" finless surfing has distinguished him as both an anachronism and forward-thinking renegade.

5 Kelly's mom worked a few years at the Islander Hut, flipping burgers and hustling to make ends meet while raising her three sons.

Caroline Marks: Sebastian was five minutes away from my house. Those are the waves I surfed every day growing up.

Sebastian Inlet is the spiritual hub of surfing in Florida, the talismanic altar where young surfers make pilgrimage. Do you remember your first time surfing there?

Kelly Slater: First time I surfed Sebastian . . . it wasn't till I was ten or eleven. I was too intimidated by the crowd. The wave was kind of intense for me. People don't understand what Sebastian was then. It was such a defined peak. The sand was always pretty good. There was always First Peak, and the way the jetty was angled, and the beach was angled, the wedge worked even on swells that had a lot of north in it. A straight north would obviously be too wedged, the angle wasn't right, but on a northeast swell, First Peak, Second Peak, and Third Peak were good. And they were all very distinct waves. You found your place in the crowd.

There was a pretty strong crew of probably thirty people who surfed there all the time and ran First Peak. [Jeff] Crawford was always part of that. But it was everyone from Lewis Graves, Jackie Grayson, Tim Briers, Kechele, both Klugels . . . Kuhn, all the Ocean Ave Crew, Bruce Walker's whole team, all the Spectrum team. There was a hierarchy in the pack. And if you weren't a local, you weren't getting waves at First Peak. Literally, the whole pack would gang mentality turn on you, be like, "Paddle down the beach! Beat it, you kook!" Even though I was a little kid, most of the time I wouldn't go to First Peak the first couple of years I surfed Sebastian.

CJ Hobgood: I mean, just going to the inlet and trying to *catch* a wave. We were on the grom bowl on the inside. There was such a group of guys. Every time Damien and I showed up for a surf contest, we would get our butts kicked, and in the group division above us, people were really good and really hungry. If you etched out a final and got like a fourth, we were like, 'woo, that was pretty sick.' All the guys you could think of were at the inlet . . . Bill Hartley, Dave Speir, Charlie Kuhn . . .

Kelly Slater: Back then, guys would just drop in and fade 'em. Now, if a kid gets a wave and you fade him, it ends up on Instagram and you get in trouble. "Oh, you won't let the kid get the wave." Back then, you had to find your place in the lineup. I don't remember my dad pushing me into a single wave, or blocking for me, or any of that stuff. You go down the beach, you surf, you find your spot in the lineup. You find your respect. And if you don't get waves, you're crying. It happened to me at Sebastian. You're too young, you're too small. If you got lucky and there was nobody on the Peak and one came, you might get it.

That localism, and that whole thing those days at Sebastian was super cool. It was a gang mentality. You had to be a local to fit in, but it really created the DNA and the roots of surfing for us. And if you were a hard-core surfer, you could become part of that group. If it was just a fun thing for you on the weekend, you didn't belong. Those old-school guys really held it down.

In 2003, the Army Corps of Engineers renovated the jetty extension and accidentally removed the majestic, warping wave of First Peak. Here's Matt Walker, writing for The Surfer's Journal ("Death of Sebastian, a Eulogy, 1969–2003") on the loss of Florida's most consistent wave: "Overnight, the pits, the power—the rabid pack and daily shit fights— disappeared."

Kelly Slater: Sebastian was a hundred million times better before [the jetty reconstruction]. It was actually a proper wave that wedged in one spot, with good angle on the wedge. Some people's theory is that it changed because they changed the jetty, but the structure of the jetty, the stuff above the water might have changed a little bit, but the angle of the jetty didn't change, as far as I know. So what happened was the beach got longer, and it got shallower outside, and so the waves break further out, and the further you go out the jetty, the more it angles to the south, and as it angles more to the south, the angle of the wedge gets much steeper, and refracts back to the north too much. So essentially, the beach got longer, and it breaks further out, and it doesn't hit the jetty the way it used to. They would have to make an extension on the north side of the jetty that angles more east, really widen the whole thing and then dredge all that sand on the outside. Boats used to anchor outside, or fish outside, say a hundred yards off the jetty. It was 30 feet deep, and now it's 15 feet deep. And waves break out by the end of the jetty all the time. When I was a kid, I don't remember waves almost ever breaking out there. Only on the biggest swells.

Caroline Marks: I actually had this conversation yesterday. Every time I go home to Florida, I see Speir, and Kechele, and all those guys, and it's crazy how good they say the wave used to be. I never really experienced that. I feel like we did get it fun enough, but it wasn't the same as it was back in the day. I would usually go down the beach and try to surf the lefts.

In 2003, the freak wave that prepped kids like Kelly and CJ for steeper, hollower reef breaks was gone. And yet Caroline would earn her chops at Sebastian, and go on to win both a world championship and an Olympic gold medal. How does that happen? Is it that Florida groms somehow sense the nuances of wave behavior—the rips, the double-ups—better than other surfers? And how does that intuition facilitate the transition to different spots around the world?

Caroline Marks: I think it takes a lot of time. Just a lot of hours in the water at different venues. A wave like Pipeline, it's already a really hard wave, and there's so many different faces of it, that you just got to spend so much time out there, and you're forever going to be learning. But the more you go out there, you get better at knowing where to sit, and what it does on different swell directions. And then you also obviously have an *instinct,* and you kind of listen to that, and you kind of have this feeling. I don't know how to explain it. You have this feeling, like, "I feel like I should paddle over here right now."

You just kinda gotta listen to that and hope you make the right decision. Really. But, you know, just a lotta hours in the water is what's going to make you better overall.

[On the tour], a lot of the waves we surf are point breaks. It definitely was an area where I had to learn and work on it. I think my strength was beach breaks for so long. I mean, it's still a big strength of mine. But I did have to work on, when I went to Bells, I went to Snapper,[6] linking a bunch of turns together, like eight turns instead of one. You know, I was used to super short period, drop in and take off, do one turn if you can; so I had to work on that area of my surfing. I grew up surfing the harder version, the quicker, kind of shorter

---

6   Bells Beach, Snapper Rocks: two of Australia's most prestigious right-hand point breaks.

© TOM DUGAN / ESM

Another liftoff from the Space Coast. CJ Hobgood, aerialist extraordinaire, Sebastian Inlet.
Photograph by Tom Dugan.

period wave. Yeah, maybe it's a Florida thing. You have to turn when you can, because you don't have much time.

Florida surfers are scrapping all the time. Does growing up with a scarcity of waves prepare you for high-intensity competition?

CJ Hobgood: Why do some people perform better under pressure than others, when it matters most? You gotta be hungry, right? But a lot of people are hungry. I think coming from Florida, you have a chip on your shoulder.

Kelly Slater: Because we did have to work so hard, and we were second- or third-class citizens when it came to the world of surfing. And there's some weird irony that a lot of Florida guys have been great big wave and/or Pipe surfers. Crawford winning Pipe back in the day. Obviously, I've had a good run there, but look at the Hobgoods, and their barrel prowess at places like Teahupo'o or Cloudbreak. Todd Holland just absolutely charging big waves. Todd Morcom, out of his mind crazy . . . and there's a whole bunch of other guys . . . guys who live down in Mexico and Costa Rica, they've become incredible barrel riders and charge big waves. Damien Hobgood was charging Nazaré . . . I think from our little community we've made a pretty profound impact around the world.

Even today, the Space Coast maintains its small-town vibe. That's rare in a surf community. You don't really find it in California. As you go up the East Coast, the towns are more rugged; they're colder. It's not summer-style beach living. So there's this small zone of temperate weather with relatively steady surf and light crowds. I saw Kelly surfing Driftwood House yesterday, a total crap day: waist-high, sideshore winds. For someone who regularly surfs the best breaks in the world, what could possibly motivate you to paddle out on a day like that?

Kelly Slater: Florida is really the only time I get to surf by myself. So even when it's shitty, if there's a little wave, I'll paddle out. I really like surfing at home. I get to surf with a couple friends. I like to catch up with Hartley, Dave Speir. I think East Coast surfers have a communion or bond that a lot of other people don't have.

CJ Hobgood: This is the perfect arc—you grow up in a small town, it's solid, it's middle-class, but there's just enough here that makes you want to split town, you know, where you're like, "Dude, I gotta get outta here." And you travel, you go and explore, and you do all these great things, and then you realize, wow, that place where I grew up is so sick, and you come back. I don't know when we'll lose it, but we still have that, "what's up, neighbor?" or "lemme grab your trash." We haven't gotten too rich, there's still not too much money, which erodes all those things.

Caroline Marks: I've been fortunate to surf the best waves in the world all year-round, but to this day, when I go home, even if it's not that good . . . I get excited when it's a north swell and the wind's blowing like 100 miles an hour down the beach and there's a lot of current. There's no one out, so it makes it fun. It's so rare to find these days. And it's tricky. You have to read the ocean. I think what makes a great surfer is not only what you can do with the board, but you have to be so good at reading the ocean.

It's crazy, because surfing is obviously my career—even though it doesn't feel like a job—but it's also my outlet. That feeling of being on the wave, that freedom, is so nice. No one can tell you what to do, there's no right or wrong way to do it, everyone's got their unique style . . . There's nothing like it . . . It's just a feeling you get. Some special connection.

<center>~~~~~</center>

To be a local of this barrier island—one of 54,000 privileged souls—is to tap into that special connection. Short-interval swells, high wave count, the ability to surf all day with your pack. Gratitude. All these factors play a role in creating a champion. But I suspect some deeper magic at work, some karmic force imprinted on these shores by those who rode before. Sebastian Inlet, that playground of angels, happens to sit atop the archaeological site of Jece, the capital town of the Ais. Is it so crazy to wonder what ancient power still haunts these waters?

On Shapers

Ocean-dwelling cultures have been catching waves since the first primitive rafts put to sea, but the practice of riding a wave while standing on two feet originated, as far as we know, in the ancient societies of Polynesia. Surfing was a religious ritual on the Hawaiian Islands, bound up in *kapu,* or their ancestral code of conduct. The shaping of the surf vessel, too, was a sacred act. Every step in the process summoned *mana,* or holy power, into the spirit of the board.

The Hawaiians built their surfboards from the trunks of the wiliwili, ula, or koa trees, scraping the wood down with basalt adz blades (the first planers), charring it with fire, rough-sanding the board with coral, then with coarse grit sand, then an even finer grit sand mixed with water. After buffing the surface to a shine with sharkskin, they would brush on a gloss coat of kukui nut oil and leave it to dry in the sun.

The longest, and most regal, of the Hawaiian surfboards was the *olo:* measuring 12–20 feet long, it weighed up to 200 pounds and was ridden exclusively by chiefs or noblemen. The midlength was called *ali'i,* or *alaia:* 7–12 feet long, *alaias* sported round noses and square tails, and had the inchoate ability to tack subtle angles across the unbroken face of waves. The smallest surfboard was the *paipo:* round-nosed and stubby, it was a bellyboard favored mostly by children, and ranged from 3–6 feet long.

By the early 1900s, Hawaiians had begun to incorporate redwood as a viable surfboard-building material. George Freeth—the Waikiki beach boy who took Jack London on his first foray into surfing, in 1907—cut down a redwood *alaia* and rode it as a lighter, more nimble option to the traditional boards. Around the same time, Freeth's friend Duke Kahanamoku (whom many regard not only as the father of modern surfing but of modern surfboard shaping), created his own model—10 feet long, 23 inches wide, 3 inches thick, and weighing in at 70 pounds. This Duke "plank" board was the precursor to the modern longboard.

Freeth and Kahanamoku toured the mainland throughout the 1910s to spread the surf gospel, and by the '20s, Californians were regularly shouldering redwood planks into breaks from Rincon to Imperial Beach. But these boards were cumbrous, unwieldy, and tended to bog down over time, so shapers began to experiment with lighter, more resilient construction methods. Tom Blake, a world-class paddleboarder and seminal surfcraft tinkerer, built his first hollow, skin-on-frame surfboard in 1929. Blake created a system of internal lightweight spruce ribs, modeled after airplane wings, and encased them in a thin veneer of African mahogany. These hollow boards (later nicknamed "cigar boxes") measured 12 feet long and were almost 4 inches thick, with a rounded nose similar to an *alaia,* and a tail pointed like the tip of an aloe leaf. At 45 pounds, they planed on the water like no surfboards before them.

In the 1930s, shapers discovered the ultralight wood of the balsa tree, which grew in abundance in the Ecuadorian rainforests. Balsa was porous and absorbed water easily—it would have been useless to the ancient Polynesians—but a new technology for mass-producing glass wool made it possible for shapers to waterproof the balsa planks by draping them with fiberglass cloth, pouring resin overtop, and squeegeeing them to a glabrous shine. A typical balsa and fiberglass longboard from the '30s and '40s was 10 feet long, with a slight rocker (or upward longitudinal curve) in its nose that allowed for steeper entry drops, and weighed about 30 pounds. Men, women, and most hale youths could carry one across the beach. And once you put it in the water, it seemed to weigh nothing at all.

But nothing would revolutionize modern surfboard design more than that epiphanic moment in 1935, when Tom Blake, that Milwaukee-born waterman, took an aluminum skeg off an old speedboat and affixed it to the underside of his surfboard. In all the thousands of years prior, surfers had ridden waves more or less straight toward shore. If they wanted to turn, they had to drop a foot into the water and lean hard on the inside rail. With Blake's innovation, the tail would hold firm as a surfer sliced freely up and down the open face without "sliding ass," or spinning out. (In time, surfboard fins would evolve toward deeper, thinner, and wider surfaces, with all manner of rakes, foils, cants, and sweeps.)

The lineups of the '40s and '50s were ruled by balsa longboards with glassed-on D-shaped fins. In Hawaii, big-wave riders George Downing

Chipping the adz blade out of a chunk of hardened basalt.

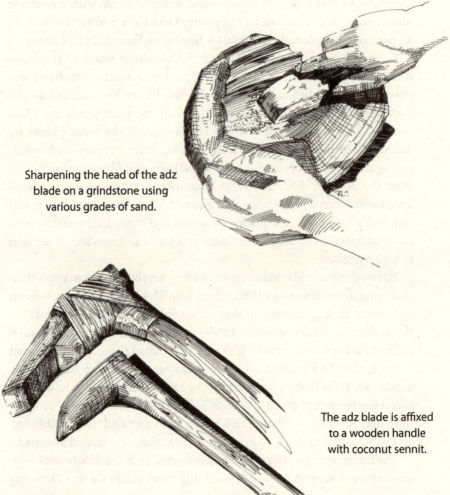

Sharpening the head of the adz blade on a grindstone using various grades of sand.

The adz blade is affixed to a wooden handle with coconut sennit.

Splitting the koa tree trunk.

Planing the raw plank with the adz blade.

Rough-sanding the deck
with a coral block.

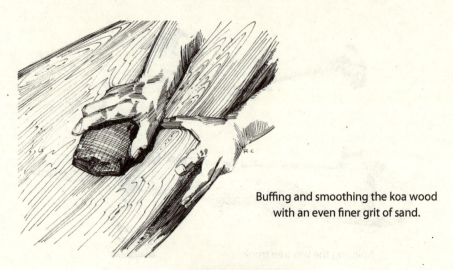

Buffing and smoothing the koa wood
with an even finer grit of sand.

Wet sanding the board with
sharkskin for a sleek finish.

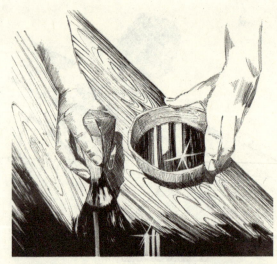

Brushing on a gloss coat of
kukui nut oil.

Artwork by Ron Croci.

and Wally Froiseth took advantage of the newfound speed and stability to tackle previously-unheard-of 20–30-foot waves at Makaha.

In California, surfers like Joe Quigg, Matt Kivlin, and Bob Simmons—looking to race ahead of the zippering point breaks of Malibu and Rincon—developed a superthin, rockered-out balsa board that looked like a potato chip. This "Malibu chip" weighed 25 pounds and became the board of choice during the *Gidget* years, that inflection point when surfing entered the American dreamscape.

The next great streamlining of surfboard materials came in the '50s, with the introduction of polyurethane foam—a firm, white, closed-cell material that could be planed, sanded, and made watertight with fiberglass and resin. Bob Simmons famously rode one of the first foam-core boards (a dual-fin, Styrofoam board sealed with plywood) in 1949, and Dave Sweet was experimenting with molded foam boards as early as '56. But polyurethane foam would not take hold as a widely used surfboard material until Hobie Alter and Gordon "Grubby" Clark developed a method for pouring their foam mixture into concrete molds and letting the blanks stiffen up under pressure. The duo would also introduce a crucial ingredient into the foam board: the center stringer, a single strip of balsa that ran down the middle and prevented the board from overflexing and snapping. In 1958, Hobie and Clark began to market their custom-made surfboards out of their surf shop in Laguna Beach. Clark would later branch off to start his own production company, Clark Foam, in 1961, and become the world's leading provider of surfboard blanks for more than four decades.

When Bill Feinberg opened up the first surfboard factory on the East Coast, Oceanside Surfboards, in Cocoa, in 1962, he had difficulty procuring foam blanks from Clark. Mike Mann, the current owner of the Longboard House in Indialantic, and one-time partner with Feinberg, explains: "Clark wouldn't sell him foam at the beginning. The Dana Point Mafia—Hobie, Hansen, Dewey—they wanted you to mail-order the boards. Didn't want anybody getting strength on the East Coast."

Cocoa Beach had positioned itself at the nexus of East Coast surfing, and Feinberg looked to become its main hometown supplier. He invited Harold Walker, another early producer of foam blanks, to Florida for a fishing trip and was able to convince him to ship his blanks to the Oceanside factory. In order to supply the top surfers with top-quality boards, Feinberg hired expert shapers and laminators from California: Johnny Rice—a Santa Cruz shaping master and student of Dale Velzy—

and Rick James and Pat O'Hare, who'd worked with Greg Noll out in Manhattan Beach.

One warm and windless night in July 1967, Feinberg's factory mysteriously erupted into flame. The *Miami Herald* ran a small story on it the next morning: "The fire and explosions blew out the roof of the 8,400-square-foot concrete building and left its concrete walls cracked and blackened. Total inventory of the firm, valued at $11,000 by owner William Feinberg, was reduced to ashes. The building was also a total loss. Cause of the fire is under investigation."

The volatile, flammable chemicals in resin make fires somewhat common occurrences in shaping factories, but ask any old-timer about the Oceanside conflagration, and he'll shake his head and drop into a hushed, insinuating tone. Those first cutthroat, Wild West years of surfboard sales in Florida are peppered with rumors of foul play. Drugs and thievery were rampant in the business. A fire here and there only added spice to the mix.

Grubby Clark did eventually start selling blanks to the East Coast—to Feinberg's main competitor, Dick Catri. (Though Catri was notorious for his hard-ass tactics, he was never linked to the alleged arson.)

Feinberg would collect his insurance money and rebuild the Oceanside factory. The blanks continued to arrive in a steady stream from California, the East Coast houses shaped and glassed them, and the kids kept ordering more. Meanwhile, Clark and Walker continued to refine the foam technology; by the mid-'60s, a stylish "poly" longboard weighed just 20 pounds, and the young riders were flinging them into dazzling new stunts and maneuvers.

For a fleeting moment in history, between 1968 and 1972, Cape Canaveral was the only place in the world where a person could hitch a direct flight onto an interstellar body.[1] Those Apollo moon shots provided mankind a view into untapped realms. It was an awakening, a shock to the system, a major mind trip. Was it any surprise, then, that the next major breakthrough in surfboard design occurred during this same period?

The shortboard revolution traces its origins to a Californian kneeboarder by the name of George Greenough. Greenough's homemade "flex-spoon" board ("Velo," he called it) was *paipo*-esque, and less than 5 feet long. Built of space-age materials, it weighed just *6 pounds*. The

---

1 Never before, and never since (as of this writing, in 2025).

deck consisted of layers of semitranslucent fiberglass, and the rails were a raised girdle of polyurethane foam. In the water, the flex spoon sprung and warped with the contortions of the wave. Greenough added a deep, raky fin styled after a bluefin tuna's dorsal, which gave him the uncanny ability to slot into the steep, vertical section of the wave, wrap turns easily back toward the whitewater, fly straight up the face, rocket down the line, or disappear completely inside the tube.

In '67, Greenough took Velo to Australia and showed it to Bob McTavish, a Queensland surfer and board builder, who was inspired to create a 7'6", 14-pound surfboard with a wedge-shaped tail and a hard chine on the bottom, like a V-bottomed boat. On it, a rider could realize drastic, swooping turns without losing speed. McTavish, along with test riders Nat Young and Wayne Lynch, would take these shorter boards out to Maui and ride Honolua Bay more critically, more freely, and more top-to-bottom than anyone before them. This style of surfing came to be known as the "involvement" school.

Hawaiian boardmaker Dick Brewer would take what the Aussies were doing a step further, and his thinner, lighter, concave-bottom designs would pioneer the new-age, acid-fueled shortboard revolution.[2] In 1970, every *Surfer* magazine cover showcased a shortboarder—either lacerating an edge in a deep, aggressive bottom turn, nestled in a sunlit barrel, or blurred out in speed frames. Clark Foam had by then begun mass-producing shortboard blanks, and in an unconventional move, Grubby Clark decided to sell his blanks at a fixed price to all comers—shops and individuals alike. Anyone with a planer was suddenly free to start their own backyard operation.

The early '70s were surfing's Age of Enlightenment. Every back street in Cocoa Beach sang with the clanging of saws and rasping of sanding blocks. Long-haired kids were carving their own templates, fashioning their own outlandish watercraft. Local surf shops became the salons, or gathering places, where underground shapers, garage builders, backyard philosophers, and groms could discourse over the newest models and fin configurations.

---

2 One of Brewer's avant-garde shapes burst onto the worldwide stage in 1968, when Reno Abellira (a world-class shaper in his own right) blew the collective mind at the World Surf Titles in Rincón, Puerto Rico, on "Le Serpent"—a 6-foot, 9-pound, deep-indigo Brewer-shaped pintail. Abellira didn't win the contest (the waves were too small for the board), but he sliced cleaner, faster lines than anyone else, and his velocity on the takeoffs further pried opened the doors of perception.

At one point, the Salick brothers' shop was the hippest spot in town, and they moved about one hundred boards a week—stingers, twin-fins, fish, lightning bolts. But in the early '80s the Salicks sold their operation, and Ocean Avenue, Quiet Flight, and Natural Art began to dominate the East Coast surfboard market. Shapers were building ever-thinner, lighter vessels, including the newly minted thruster design.[3]

To be hired by one of the top shaping houses was to be initiated into a secret kung fu school. An apprentice would begin by sweeping foam dust, then work his way up to polishing, then sanding. The talent pool ran extra deep in Brevard County, and the list reads like a roster of shaping hall-of-famers: Mike Tabeling, Richard Price, Steve Holloway of Lightwave Surfboards, Regis Jupinko (the original owner of Quiet Flight before he sold to Jim and Ed Leasure), Bill Eberwein (laminator par excellence), Doug Wright of Rainbow Surfboards, Robert Strickland, Kurt and Jim Wilson, Allen White, Jeff Haney at Ocean Image, Bill Vollmer of Little Hawaii surf shop, Larry Pope (a legendary surf photographer who could sand sixty-four boards a day), Freddie Grosskreutz and Bob Seeback (the highest-skilled guys at the highest-skilled job—glassing), Dennis O'Hare (Pat's brother, one of the world's finest pin liners, working freehand with a cigarette dangling from his mouth), Claude Codgen of Sunshine Surfboards, Jim Phillips (Jim the genius, his shop next door to O'Hare's on Manatee Lane), Tommy Maus, Donny Mulhern of MTB, Loehr, Munson, Kechele, Tom Neilson, Stu Sharpe, Chris Birch, Jesse Fernandez, Ricky Carroll (the guru of all modern-day gurus), Bruce Regan, Rich Rudolph, Bill Johnson, Sean Slater, Joe Johnson, Joey Maus . . .

On December 5, 2005, a day that would come to be known as "Blank Monday," Grubby Clark shocked the surf world when, without warning, he shuttered his doors and declared the end of Clark Foam. It was as if the fragrant cloud of chocolate smoke had suddenly stopped wafting from Wonka's factory. Clark was cryptic about his reasons for the abrupt shutdown, alluding to some concerns about the EPA and government

---

3 Thruster: In 1981, the shortboard market shifted gears after Simon Anderson—a Sydney-born power surfer—created the three-fin thruster design. The fins were smaller than on the twins, but on the turns, the center fin assisted, grabbing the face of the wave and giving the surfer more thrust. The thruster would become the standard shortboard setup for the next forty years.

regulations.[4] Though no formal investigation was under way, Clark ordered his team to destroy all his concrete molds and break down the equipment, leaving the surfboard industry high and dry.

In the mad scramble to fill the void left by Clark Foam's shutdown, surf shops began ordering heavily flawed blanks from lower-quality producers. Clark had kept his foam consistent and reliable; he had let the mix set up in such a way as to make the deck denser than the bottom, which allowed shapers a special feel and technique with the hand planer. Now shapers had to deal with air pockets and gaps in the mixture and struggled mightily to produce consistent product.

Surf shops found it harder to justify buying local-made boards, which had become both more expensive and less reliable. Out of desperation, they turned to Chinese imports (known as "pop-outs," for the speed of their production), cheap, soulless replicas of classic boards but good enough for box stores and the clueless masses.

Another effect of Grubby Clark's dropout was the proliferation of new materials and technologies. The most ubiquitous of these was a new breed of foam—expanded polystyrene, or EPS. Lighter and less dense than polyurethane, EPS boards were glassed with epoxy resin instead of polyester resin and gave the rider a floatier feel underfoot. They were more user-friendly for beginner surfers and provided added lift for high-performance aerialists. The EPS blanks were challenging, at first, to shape by hand, but with the advancement of CNC (computer numerical control) machines, shapers with enough capital could cut consistent and high-precision shapes, indistinguishable from handmade shapes except for their artificial symmetry and perfection of line.

And yet, for certain people sensitive to such deviations, something was missing from these machine-shaped boards. Some feeling, some alchemic spark didn't translate into the watercraft. For those increasingly rare Jedis who chose to persist in the traditional methods and build surfboards by hand, from start to finish, US Blanks would eventually replace Clark Foam as a domestic supplier of old-style poly blanks.

---

4   A little-discussed topic in the surf world is the environmental impact of polyurethane foam construction, the "original sin" of the modern board-building industry. Foam is composed of a toxic petrochemical—toluene diisocyanate—and the polyester resin used to waterproof it is a carcinogen and a biohazard. When a foam board dies, it is not easily disposable, or recyclable. Nor is any of the process ecologically responsible.

The fact that it is nearly impossible to get rich shaping surfboards does not deter the devout. A shaper is the type of person who infatuates over a sanding block or a well-worn wooden caliper, whose hands are instruments of faith, and who works, like the craftsmen of old, within a thousandth of an inch. Just as the ancient Polynesians lovingly cupped their well-worn adz blades, the modern hand-shaper caresses their Skil 100 planer, lays their soul into it, and imparts their *mana* into the vessel.

Thickness Flow

~~~~~~~~~~

The Larry Mayo Perspective

I met Larry Mayo while surfing at the Driftwood House, that old wooden
cracker shack down in south Cocoa Beach. It was sometime around 2012.
I was riding a McTavish Fireball, a Thailand-built 9'6" with too much rocker
to noseride worth a damn. I'd just caught a longish left into the beach
when Mayo asked whose boards I rode. No one had ever put the question
to me quite like that before.

I had seen his surfboards around town, had long admired his work.
I ordered my first custom board from him that night. Little did I realize
how much a custom shape, built by a local shaper familiar with your own
style, could change your life.

Larry Mayo became my guru, my confidante, my gateway into the mystic.
I've been riding his boards ever since.

Blank.

Somewhere at the southern edge of Cocoa Beach, Larry Mayo takes his
caliper to a slab of US Blanks foam. The shaper—tanned, green-eyed,
gloriously rustic, handsome in the way of the northern Italian paisano
or the Frenchman of Provence—is about the same size as the blank. "The
classic 6'2" C fish blank," Mayo says. "Blue foam." The face of the slab is
factory shorn, rough, pitted. Mayo skids his hands over it. Somewhere
in this block of foam, a stub-tail diamond quad is hiding.

Mow.

Mayo's planer drones like a siren, stings the ears. He cross-steps, barefoot, through two passes, blending his cut bands. "Flat rocker," he says.

"Fast and wide." He checks his notes. "The kid wants three logos on the deck." For some reason, this amuses Mayo.

Outline.

Mayo is shaper, sander, glasser, hot coat man. He laminates, tints, tapes, pin lines, embeds his own fin boxes. He pencil-marks the stringer, pulls in an eighth, lets out like a bespoke tailor. Traces curves along Masonite. Marries templates. "It will go," he says. "Get on a plane quick." Behind the jigsaw, foam dust on his arms and his feet, he shears away the edges until only the board remains.

Sand.

"Turns out Greenough was right all along," Mayo says. "You fit the board to the wave." Foiling the vessel, peeling it clean as apple flesh. Student of the old new school. Take what you've learned and move on. At the Milwaukee grinder, sweeping it in flourishes, Mayo smooths the deck to fuzz, shaves stringer, curls wood, blends and blends until it is sleek as eggshell.

Cloth.

In a corrugated, mangrove-fringed marina on the Banana River, the glassing room has the look of a dojo: minimalist, clean, razor blades in the wall like throwing stars. "Another burgundy board," Mayo says, unspooling the six-ounce Volan over his most recent sculpture. "Just when it stopped looking like a crime scene in here." His scissors are a foot long. He slices the cloth with wrist-driven cuts.

Glass.

Coke-bottle greens, persimmons, saffrons, mosses. His tint jobs breed collectors, inspire fetishism. Straining the burgundy now, gentling it like a sommelier, Mayo meditates on viscosity and proportion. In respirator and rubber gloves, he slicks his squeegee over his fish. Fresh-air fans inject cold air. He wants the foam contracting as he lacquers the resin over the Volan. This takes time. This is what Mayo Surfboards are about: time. The extra pass.

Hot Coat.

The crest of County Mayo, Ireland, features a rockered-out ship aroll on blue waves. His forebears, a maritime people. For his own shield, he

Larry Mayo, running the resin.

Photograph courtesy of Larry Mayo.

employs a circle of psychedelic, cloud-patterned letters. Jimi Hendrix meets *The White Album*. He papers a single logo over the stringer. Elegant enough. Mayo does not put three logos on a deck.

A 4-inch paintbrush for the hot coat. As if resin is pouring from his fingertips. The color resurrects. "The closer you get to the old school way," he says, "the better the job."

Gloss.

Mayo has made it perfect, then sanded it down again. The board now has the matte finish of a Red Delicious apple. "You have to sand deep into the hot coat to get good clarity on the gloss coat," he says. A lost art in a spray-finish age, the gloss coat—a residual of artisanal times, of muscle cars, Stratocasters.

Mayo pulls the hardener up through a straw with a chemist's touch. "A voodoo to glossing. It's volatile. You can't have oils or contaminants on the brush." He eases it on in long, sinuous strokes, the final coat, brings the board to an impossible, seductive shine. A '71 Porsche. "It's good when it locks up like that." Mayo smiles. "Right after it flows out."

Polish.

Mayo takes a grinder to the board, sands down the gloss coat with 320-grit Rhinolux paper. Switches out to 400 and hits it again. Sands it yet again with the 600. Mayo's hands have passed over every inch of this board, by my count, forty-three times.

He blows the board clean, ties on his apron, brushes on the polish like an old country woodworker. Forty-four.

The buffer clocks around at 6,000 rpm, riding the deck to Wilco's "Whole Love." The surfboard fulfills its own destiny. Mayo is just here to see it through. The true and final color: a vintage burgundy, pure and clean, sheened to mirror glass.

Mayo's reflection swims inside as he cross-steps into another pass.

George Robinson

~~~~~~~~~~~~~~~~~~~~~

The True Line

The shaper formerly known as George Robinson looks too thickly alive, too vital for a man who has been planing timber and sanding rails for forty-six years. Sturdy, Incan, hickory-haired, meaty in the hands, he leads me beneath a curtain of sea grapes and tells me he is contemplating a return to the Ecuadorian spelling of his name.

In most respects, Jorge Robinson's shaping space recalls the workshops of other master surfboard builders, with pleasant variations: where foam particles usually film the floor, here a feathery sawdust collects. Carpenter's implements crowd the walls: bar clamps, scales, hand planers. Also, there is this sweet, earthy scent of wood shavings.

A longboard—honey-blond balsa, a triple stringer—is up on the racks, gleaming like an enchantment. After the tide drops, I will paddle it out. I've never surfed a balsa board before. Jorge encourages me to pick it up. The thing jumps from the racks. "Fifteen pounds," he tells me. "That's solid wood. No chambers."

The glossed grain summons Edwards, Velzy, Hobie, Jacobs, and Simmons—young American revolutionaries who used balsa to change the way surfers approached wave riding. Balsa reigned during the transitional period between the 80-pound *olo* and the lightweight foam blank. It was a short-lived era. As soon as Grubby Clark industrialized the surfboard building process, balsa surfboards began to seem rustic and old-timey, objects to be cherished by purists, collectors, or folk artists.

Ninety-five percent of the world's balsa is harvested in Ecuador, from forests at the base of the Andes, near the tributaries of the Guayas River. Native Ecuadorians navigated these waterways and fished from balsawood rafts centuries before the Spanish named the tree "balsa," which is the Spanish word for "raft." The trees (*Ochroma pyramidale*)—lucent-leaved, gray-skinned—proliferate only in the windless lowlands of the tropical rainforests, where they sprout like weeds. Their cells are 90 percent water, and though they can grow to over 100 feet tall, they shoot up too fast, apparently, to form tree rings.

In 1972, the shaper formerly known as George Robinson opened Ecuador's first surf shop—Mar Bravo—and became the most uncommon of specimens in the industry: a production shaper of balsa surfboards. Since then, he estimates he has built 2,500 balsa boards. His "shaper's family tree" is simple enough: he learned the craft from Johnny Rice, who learned from Velzy, who learned from Blake, who learned from Duke Kahanamoku, who took his direction from the Source.

Wood has life. It is not uniform. Every piece has a soul and a history. To find the thickest, lightest balsa—*la embra*, as they call it—Jorge orders his wood rough-sawn instead of milled. He takes advantage of the natural curvature of the planks to cut his rocker templates, does some mild chambering, and glues up from the T-band first, to get it true. You don't want it to twist, he tells me. To spring. To bend. He clamps the blank together, leaves it to dry in the sun. Only then does he arrive at the point where other shapers begin their process. Foiling the wood requires more fastidiousness than foam. You can't walk the board evenly or take a screen to the rails. You need a razor-blade block plane instead of a surform. And you must step back constantly to size it up.

"But it will outlive ten foam boards," Robinson says. "And it won't knee dent." If the resin shatters, you can sand down to the bare wood and get it looking like new. The cost of a balsa board might be double the cost of a foam board, but the craft could very well last forever.

The durability of any species lies in its ability to adapt. In this sense, it is not surprising that George Robinson is willing to take a new name so late in life. But what is he changing, really? Just the spelling—the essence remains the same. They have called him Jorge in the Republic of the Equator—the center stringer of the Earth—for years.

The tide has gone out. It's time to give Jorge's board a go. On the paddle out, it cuts the water with a stiff buoyancy. No flop. No flutter. The board generates an easier sort of momentum.

As I take off on my first wave of the day, I feel a deepening connection to ancient, invisible traditions. There is less flex, less bounce down the face. The sensation is so easy to express: wood takes a truer line than foam.

Ricky Carroll

~~~~~~~~~~~~~~~~

Portrait of a Grandmaster

Viewed from the roadside, the R&D surfboard factory in Rockledge looks like a modest, unembellished warehouse building. There is no signage out front, nothing to indicate what product might be manufactured within its walls, but a lightness suffuses the air all around it, an Arcadian peacefulness somehow out of place in this industrial setting. The clouds seem painted on the sky by some Dutch Golden Age master. A mockingbird pipes a woodwind song from the slash pines. As I approach the front door, I am overcome by that flutter of wonder and awe I always feel when entering a sacred space.

Ricky Carroll is the perhaps most celebrated surfboard shaper on the East Coast today. He's built high-performance shortboards for the top tier of the professional ranks—the Hobgood brothers, Danny Melhado, Cheyne Horan, Larry Bertlemann—and custom longboards for logging mavens like Bonga Perkins, Jesse Restivo, and Justin Quintal.[1] For more than thirty years, Ricky's RC line of boards have commanded respect and envy at surf spots from Miami up to Rhode Island.

Insofar as a master's skill can be judged by his performance in head-to-head matchups against other masters, Ricky has consistently tri-

---

1   Quintal, yet another world-title surfer from Florida (Jacksonville), is further proof of the precept: *the best in Florida can be the best anywhere*. Quintal was crowned WSL longboard world champion in 2019; more impressively, he won the most prestigious longboard competition in the world, the Duct Tape Invitational, *ten times*, more than any other surfer, while riding Ricky Carroll boards. He and Ricky have since collaborated on the "Black Rose" line of surfcraft.

umphed over the world's best. Since 2007, an elite group of shapers have gathered at the Boardroom Show in Del Mar, California, to compete in the Grand Kumite of surfboard shaping contests—the Icons of Foam Shape-off. The shapers lay hands on a classic surfboard and step into glass booths, where they have ninety minutes alone with a chunk of foam, and the task to re-create the surfboard by eye and feel. Spectators cluster at the walls as the shapers box-step around the blanks, vaporizing foam until their booths look like snow globes. When the hour and a half is up, the judges inspect the fresh-cut facsimiles, placing templates over the decks and assessing the minutiae of the rails and foils. The most accurate replica is declared the winner. Of the four Icons of Foam Shape-offs Ricky Carroll entered, he won three—the inaugural contest in 2007, then again in 2008 and 2012—wielding the planer against the highest-level black belts in the business, legends like Chris Christenson, Wayne Rich, and Reno Abellira.

I open the factory door and am greeted by the high, mellow, whistling drone of distant planers. A girl folding T-shirts in the front room smiles and directs me up a flight of stairs. I climb slowly, reverently. At the top, the sun filters through amber skylights and illuminates the grandmaster himself, standing among rows of his objets d'art—glistening poly longboards in Tyrian purple, seafoam green, and cobalt blue, pristine Takayama Model T's, and gloss-coated single-fin eggs bearing the "Black Rose" emblem.

Ricky has a Polynesian look: ringlets of dark hair swimming down his back, and the robust forearms and calves of a Major League third baseman. There is a wariness in his expression that borders on the angelic, the look of a man who has attained perfection at something but does not particularly care to discuss it. He is supposedly sixty-four years old, though he seems too untouched by time, too smooth and comfortable in his own skin to be much older than forty-five. He reminds me of someone from my past, though I can't quite place who it is. I study his face a bit too long, trying to recall.

Every great shaper begins their journey as a great surfer. Ricky is no exception to this rule. He came up surfing in Satellite Beach in the early '70s, on the same stretch of beach where the Hobgood twins would learn to surf, and where Matt Kechele and company would brave the infamous Halloween Swell of 1991. Like all Satellite Beach groms, Ricky rode his bike to the beach, and every day he would pass by the house of Mary

Ann Hayes—an East Coast Surfing Hall of Famer[2]—who was shaping surfboards out in her carport.

"I stopped in a few times to watch her," Ricky tells me. "She glassed them, built the whole board right there at her house. I was like, 'I want to do that.' Out of necessity. My brother and I shared a board. I was thirteen years old. So I found a longboard that was in the trash at the beach, broken in half, and I took the nose piece home and stripped all the glass off, and shaped myself a board. I just used a surform[3] and a sanding block. It was very crude."

It seems appropriate, in this origin story, that the grandmaster's first teacher would be a woman. There is a suppleness, a feminine power running through the contours of every Ricky Carroll board. His glass jobs are especially graceful, cool and polished as the surface of a pearl, or the inner aperture of a conch.

Ricky surfed competitively as a teenager, traveling up to North Carolina every year to compete in the ESA (Eastern Surf Association) amateur championships in the Outer Banks. He trained formally as an auto mechanic, but the contest schedule made it impossible to keep a day job. A friend, Bob Rohmann, invited him to help out at Natural Art at night, sweeping up and fixing dings, and paid him cash on the side. Pete Dooley, the owner of the shop, wasn't aware of the new kid but would often come in early to see boards that had giant gouges in them the day before repaired as if by magic, like in the story of the shoemaker and the elves. By the time Dooley learned about Ricky and offered him a job as a polisher, the student coolly informed the head of the dojo he had already been working at Natural Art for a year.

We are standing in a sort of clerestory, overlooking R&D's inner factory. Stacked on shelves against one of the walls are hundreds of curved strips of Masonite—rocker templates, organized by length—from 5'0" up to 10'0". These templates are the secret, ancient texts of the master shaper; perfected over the ages. Some originated from Bing, Velzy, Noll,

---

2   Mary Ann nearly became the Space Coast's first world champion at the 1972 World Championships in San Diego, where she came up one point short of Sharron Weber, of Hawaii, in a hotly contested final heat.

3   Surform: a perforated metal tool resembling a cheese grater, used to shave wood, drywall, or, in this case, polyurethane foam. It leaves a coarse, unfinished surface but provides quick, controlled, dustless removal of the material.

or Takayama designs; others were developed through years of refinement or were simply born by happy accident.

Ricky floats ahead of me, into the glue-up room, where blanks are sliced by hot wire, then sandwiched over the stringers with wooden clamps. It suddenly strikes me—Doc-Fai Wong! The grandmaster of the Choy Li Fut kung fu school on Taraval Street, in San Francisco. Both men carry their heads in the same distinctive way, unwavering, perfectly balanced, as if hovering over the body, independent of the movement of the torso and limbs.

I follow him down another set of stairs, into the main workshop area. Shaping factories tend toward the shambolic—air blowers dangling from curly yellow hoses, shop-vac power cords twisting and tripping up the eye, tilted cans of resin tint, scraps of loose wood, foam dust collecting on every surface—but at R&D a sense of order prevails. Not a thing seems out of place. There are four shaping bays, with long tube lights on the side walls for spotting imperfections, two sanding rooms with giant exhaust fans, a polishing room coated in a fluff of gray vellum, an airbrush room with improvised abstract art on the walls. In the corridor: a rack of pure white, freshly sanded boards waiting to be laminated.

When I press Ricky to estimate the number of surfboards he's built in his lifetime, he guesses he's hand-shaped about sixty thousand. Only the top shapers can crank out a finished board in less than an hour. Ricky works faster than most, averaging forty minutes per board. This would put him at about forty thousand shaping hours, all told. In the book *Outliers,* the author Malcolm Gladwell suggested that any artist, athlete, musician, or elite professional must devote ten thousand hours to their craft to attain mastery. By this standard, Ricky Carroll has practiced enough to be a master four times over.

His first intensive training came at Natural Art, where he studied under Greg Loehr and Richard Price, who were the resident senseis at the time. "Watching Greg shape was mind-blowing at that age," Ricky says. "To see what he could do with the planer. That was before what they would call the 'close-tolerance' blanks.[4] When those blanks came out, it

---

4   Close-tolerance blanks: Clark Foam was continually fine-tuning its methodology and came out with these blanks in the '80s, which were poured with rocker and foil already built in.

made it a lot easier for guys to shape shortboards. You really didn't have to take a lot of foam off. The rockers were there."

His arrangement with Dooley was simple enough: Ricky could surf all day and come in at night to shape. In his spare time, he took unused blanks and built a few boards from start to finish, cutting, planing, sanding, and laminating them himself, then leaving them on the horses for Dooley to inspect in the morning. Dooley was bewildered—the kid was shaping flawless diamonds. It wasn't long before he offered Ricky his own line—Sea Shapes.

"That was before the thruster," Ricky explains. "We were doing a lot of glass-on twin-fins. Short, wide boards. You had a wide square tail on it, or a round pin, or a wing." For the next twelve years, Ricky churned out ten to twelve boards a night, every night. Surfers started recognizing his name on the label, and he became one of the most sought-after shapers on the East Coast.

In 1992, Ricky would leave Natural Art and team up with Dusty Simmons to start R&D Surfboards. Local Motion, a popular surfboard brand out of Hawaii, heard Ricky had set out on his own, and signed him to their Florida contract. R&D moved into their current location and, for the first few years, produced a steady output of three or four hundred Local Motions a year.

"We didn't shape a single longboard for years," Ricky says. But in the early '90s, longboards were coming back into fashion. The ESA ran its inaugural longboard contests, and surfers began returning to the classic form, especially in regions where smaller, softer waves prevailed. "The longboard thing was creeping stronger and stronger."

Constructing longboards requires a bigger blank, more resin, more fiberglass, and more time under skilled hands. A shaper can finish four clear shortboards—spray, sand, and finish—in the same time it takes to build one polish-gloss longboard. Ricky sensed the changing market and began to shift toward high-quality craftsman pieces—fun shapes, longer and wider boards. "It was hard to sell a shortboard and make money. We saw these longboards with all the colors and pin lines, and you could charge more for that."

In his thirties, Ricky started riding longboards and immediately began winning contests. (Transitioning from a shortboard to a longboard is far easier than the reverse.) He traveled to Costa Rica to compete in the Rabbit Kekai longboard contest in '94 and surfed in the first heat against two eminent shapers—Claude Codgen and Donald Takayama.[5] Ricky won the heat (dubbed by the announcers "the shaper heat"). "I think I got a little respect from Donald from that," Ricky says. Takayama was as impressed by Ricky's surfboard as he was by his surfing, and he consigned R&D to build all of his East Coast boards. Just as Pat O'Hare had shaped for Greg Noll back in the '60s, Ricky became Takayama's man on the East Coast.

There was one marked difference in the relationship. Takayama had, by this time, begun utilizing the CNC machine, and his blanks were rough-shaped in California before being shipped to Florida. The surfboards arrived at R&D already cut with precise template, rocker, rail, and thickness flow dimensions. But the surfaces were still striated with computer-cut ridges, so R&D had to perform the final rubout by hand. Ricky assigned Tommy Maus—who had trained in California with Takayama—to oversee this luxury longboard line. The glasswork and resin tints were immaculate, and the product was indistinguishable from the finest Model T's and In the Pinks[6] sold on the West Coast.

In a recent interview with the Florida Surf Museum, Ricky defended his use of the CNC machines, which are regarded by some old-school shapers as soulless proxies for the human touch: "The machine can take a surfboard and copy it exactly. You can modify it in the handshape process, or in the programming process, by tweaking the numbers. It has been a good learning tool. You take your shape as a starting point, manipulate it, see what you have, build the board, ride it, and then go back to starting point A, or even go off in another direction. The machine can teach you things that you don't even know about as a hand shaper."

But the machine is no substitute for true insight, or fluency in the form. "That takes years," Ricky cautions. "Somebody that's dreaming to be a shaper has to be passionate and willing to put time in with the planer in their hand, not the machine. Shaping is like sculpting. It's a

5   Donald Takayama: A shaping legend who belongs on the Mount Rushmore of shapers (along with Duke, Blake, and Velzy), Takayama began shaping professionally at the age of thirteen, designing rides for all-time classicists like Joey Cabell, Miki Dora, and Joel Tudor. Takayama created some of the modern era's most iconic longboards: the Bing Nuuhiwa model, the Weber Performer, and the Model T.

6   Two of Takayama's top-selling models.

subtractive process. You start with this blank and you shape it down into a form. There's a lot that goes into it that's science, and there's a lot that goes into it that's feel."

Ricky leads me out a back door and across a courtyard, where a couple of lithe, middle-aged surfers are cutting pressure-treated lumber for a stage they are building out front, a future venue for live music and surf movies. The mockingbird is still singing, between the chimes of the chop saw. We arrive at an outer sanctuary with lofty, gymnasium-style ceilings—R&D's laminating building. Twenty horses are set up at even intervals across the expansive floor, which is blanketed with a thick layer of crushed coquina (a simpler, more efficient cleanup option than tar paper). Lying horizontally atop each horse is a surfboard, looking like a bushido sword on offer.

Two men in ventilator masks are prowling the floor. One slides from board to board, trimming fiberglass laps with a razor blade. The other is urging fresh resin over a deck. Ricky maintains a staff of fifteen full-time employees at R&D, no small feat in modern times, as foreign pop-outs are laying waste to most local surfboard houses. It's heartening to see a custom surfboard manufacturer surviving, preserving that crucial symbiosis between riders and shapers.

Perhaps it is the faintly toxic sting in my nostrils, or the glare of the tube lights, but I feel suddenly disoriented, lightheaded . . . one of the longboards, a crimson-edged beauty, begins to tremble and glow, like some holy artifact, a ruby-carved lotus in the heart of the monastery . . . the air shimmers around it, and the surfboard levitates . . . actually rises a few inches above the horse, hangs there, throbbing. I take a step or two backward and glance at Ricky Carroll's face. His expression reveals nothing. He is calm, dispassionate, exactly like grandmaster Doc-Fai Wong watching over his tai chi students as they practice their forms.

Here, in his place of preparation, art resolves into function. All is balance. All is harmony.

One Summer Day

Florida summers are like molasses . . . thick, hot, dripping. The birds slouch, the yard is overgrown with bougainvillea and wild, exotic grasses, the mosquitoes swarm, and a bright, languorous mist hangs over every-thing. It is stifling outside, your car feels like an oven, the sweat runs into your eyes, the sand burns your feet, the no-see-ums gnaw inces-santly at your legs. In a sort of reverse-hibernatory instinct, you want to hide away, tuck yourself into the air-conditioning, and wait for the wretched thing to play itself out.

Days stretch out like taffy, pulling, lengthening, but give no hint of snapping. Your only reprieve is to walk dazedly to the ocean and look for waves. Each time you mount the dunes, an irrational hope swells up in your chest . . . but these are Atlantic doldrum days, and summer prevails yet again. Your dreams of surf melt like candlewax over the flat, oil-slick sea.

When was the last time you surfed? It might have been a week ago, maybe two . . . no, you remember it now . . . a low front spun up the coast last month and sent a few waves in, waist- to chest-high on the sets with light north winds. High tide was the call, with cruisy lefts breaking over the inside sandbar.

This is what life has come to now . . . remembering the old times. On these slow, wistful, daydreamy days of summer, what else to do but dream and remember?

Come take a seat with me, up here on the crossover railing . . . I know it's hot; surrender to it . . . cast your eyes out over the water, to the dark mirages on the horizon, and allow the scene to dissolve into blue. I'll even raise a pensive finger to my lips, à la one of those old Bruce Brown surf flicks, and add a voice-over for effect:

"When it gets like this, it's easy to mistake the Atlantic for the last of the Great Lakes. Poor Dan . . . he's stuck down here in Flatsville while his buddies are catching an epic south swell in Malibu. 'Hey man, don't worry!' a local grom calls out, trying to sound cheerful, 'They say it's supposed to get up to shin-high tomorrow!'"

What else is there to do in such mournful times (as the German tourists slowly fill up the kiddie pool) but shake your head and hearken back to better times . . .

It was another August day, some years back, a day not unlike this one. Todd—my wild-eyed friend from the Topanga days, now living up in Manhattan—called with some exciting news.

"Hey man! Montauk's getting a swell in. Joel invited me to go surfing with him tomorrow. It's supposed to glass off in the afternoon."

"Joel?"

"Yeah, he's got plenty of boards up there."

"Joel Tudor?"

"That's what I said, bro. You should come up."

"What, catch a plane?"

"Why not? There's nothing going on in Florida."

I told Brittany that, for a longboarder, surfing with Joel Tudor would be like a golfer playing a round with Tiger Woods, or a cyclist riding with Lance Armstrong. She smiled with understanding and a bit of pity. I flew up to LaGuardia that very night.

Todd and Joel Tudor met me at Penn Station the next morning, and we caught the Jitney together out to Montauk. When I mentioned I was from Cocoa Beach, Joel said he once surfed the Driftwood House with Sean Slater, and told a story about getting chewed out by Kelly for not wearing a leash and fooling around during a Pipe contest. Once we were out of the city, we opened up the windows and tasted the sea air. The Hamptons were a fairyland of flowers and glittering sunlight and cool wind stirring the conifers. I felt impossibly light, adrift above the surface of reality. A beautiful, long-haired boy of nineteen or twenty met us at the station in Montauk and drove us along the tree-lined avenues to a sprawling white house wrapped in Japanese snowbells and azaleas.

A commune of hippies had overrun the house for the summer. They sunned their young bodies on the porch, played guitar, laughed, ate, smoked aromatic weed, slept on the outdoor furniture. They were generally pleased to see us but couldn't care less who strolled in or out, so exhausted were they from partying and lovemaking and surfing all day. The boy who had driven us from the station brought us around to the backyard, where fifteen or so longboards lay on the grass, rails glinting in the sun . . . Takayama, Weber, Hap Jacobs, Yater, Hynson . . .

Joel stepped lightly among the boards, lifting them up by the noses and trying to figure out whose was whose. He set aside a 12-foot stand-up paddleboard for himself, picked out a big, blue soft-top for Todd, and handed me a 9'6" OP Joel Tudor model—"his board," as he called it.

We walked the quarter mile to the beach, whistling and humming. The day was warm and dry, ideal weather, with only the occasional high cloud accentuating the sky in random, painterly brushstrokes. Joel pointed out a run-down old van that belonged to Allan Weisbecker, the lunatic author of one of my favorite books, *In Search of Captain Zero*. We walked barefoot, with our wetsuit tops dangling from our waists. No one worried about a thing, no one cared—we were content and blissed-out and alive.

If I never see Saint Peter pry open the gates of heaven for me, my first vision of the waves at Ditch Plains will have to serve as a replacement. I will hold it up as a respectable one at that. Long, long lefts were forming out by the rocks, curling around the point, and bowling through all the way into the beach. A golden armada of longboarders patrolled the outside, carving fluid, drop-kneed bottom turns, then stepping gracefully to the nose. One couple was tandem surfing, catching outside bombs and pumping down the line, the girl laughing and screaming from the front of the board.

We stretched our muscles among the young, summering couples on the sand, zipped up, and set out across the rocks into the cool bliss of the ocean. And what a session it was. I remember sitting on the outside, admiring the contours of the coastline, when a head-high A-frame caught me by surprise. I took off right, Todd went left. At the end of the ride, I looked down the beach. We must have been a half mile apart. As I paddled out, there was Joel, manifesting on the outside in his baseball cap, slicing across the face of a perfect left, stepping to the nose, hanging ten over, all the while casually grasping the oar in one hand.

It was what summers were supposed to be—a mellow crowd, a classic swell, friends in the water.

Now, as the music fades away and Joel's slow-motion noseride dissolves into blue, I head back down the Cocoa Beach crossover, wiping the sweat from my eyes, needing a cold drink.

These are doldrum days.

There's always the next tropical storm. And maybe, just maybe, like the grom said, it'll "get up to shin-high tomorrow."

Thoughts on
the Cold-Water Season

~~~~~~~~~~~

This piece originally appeared in the *Beachside Resident* in the winter of 2010. Our son, Kirin, was a year and a half old, and our daughter, Aubrey, was three. Brittany was frequently traveling to Los Angeles for yoga teacher training, and I would remain at home for three or four days at a time, tending to the infants.

Another morning: the cream snakes into the coffee, purls, disperses in pools of white oil. Cormorants gather at the river's edge, necks retracted, mute black sentinels of the dawn. Faraway clouds range the horizon like coral mountains.

When the boy wakes up, he is moaning, half-inhabiting his dreams. His diaper is full, his eyes puffed, his hair damp with sweat. He makes sweet, sad sounds in the Daddy's arms. The girl is awake, already dressed for the day, quietly fussing with her unicorn, her matted yellow bear. On her blanket: plastic cakes, fruits, a teapot, tiny pink spoons.

The dog tugs at the double stroller. The Daddy sighs wistfully at the low moon, fragile and lucent as wet paper on the sky. He recalls Biarritz . . . the shallow, crystalline rivers flowing through the sand at low tide, the great channel-cut rock behind the Hôtel du Palais, warm baguettes, Egyptian blue water, and those tanned French bodies, so unlike the cool, white-skinned Parisians. The girl sings softly, flutters her hands to some silent, internal symphony.

The Daddy wonders why, on this particular morning, he should be pushing a stroller. Momentarily he experiences the emasculation of the stay-at-home father: I should be hunting, he thinks, or chopping firewood. An osprey cuts across the sky. The bird is a comfort to the Daddy, somehow.

November, and the beginning of the nor'easters. Onshore winds, frigid water, open lineups, jellyfish plumes. Wetsuits flipped inside out, inspected for spiders. Weeks upon weeks of rideable wind chop. The double stroller reaches the crest in the road. The wind blows back the children's hair. Their laughter plays like piccolo music. The dog jerks at the leash. The salt air quickens the Daddy's heart. He rises on his toes . . . boyish, hopeful.

The tide is too high, the wind too strong, the waves too small. Florida's classic afflictions. The Daddy squints into the sun, mind-surfing the shorebreak. Purple spots spin in the boy's eyes, and he cries out. One last wave collapses to shore before the Daddy turns the stroller homeward: the children at peace in his long shadow. The plumeria leaves are crinkling at the edges; a few lie brown and crumpled on the grass, the first burnt vessels of winter. Again the Daddy wonders at his station in the world . . . tending to infants, mixing formula, wiping bums.

The front yards are littered with political signs: red-and-blue striped, banded with stars. Packaged and decorated like candy. Don John. Ritch Workman. Frank Sullivan. As if by name, font, and color scheme, one might peer into the character of a candidate. The Daddy has no taste for politics. It is enough to know the Democrats are asses and the Republicans white elephants. The Tea Party uses the Gadsden flag and the rattlesnake, but the Daddy envisions them more as turkeys, strutting around in costume, clucking at their feed.

At naptime, he punches "turkey" into Wikipedia and discovers a quote from Ben Franklin citing the "bad moral character" of the eagle and extolling the advantages of the turkey as the national bird. The Daddy wonders if this imagery might appeal to the Tea Party. He lies down on the couch, begins to float . . . picturing himself as the bright-eyed boy in the old family VHS movies, bounding on the sectional with skinny legs, forest-themed wallpaper guarding this ethereal world, his Buster Brown haircut bobbing up and down. The '80s are rhapsodic to him: roller rinks, *Rocky III,* hot tubs, teased hair, aviator sunglasses . . . but the boy is awake now, whimpering in his crib, and the Daddy loses this train of thought.

The Space Shuttle Discovery launches from the Earth that afternoon. The children stand immobile as garden gnomes on the grass, their heads tilted northeast. A sound like drawn-out thunder rolls in long after the boy has already lost interest. The girl remains immobile, her mouth slightly open, watching the cloudstring coil and drift. When the white star disappears, the engines are still booming. Her hands close upon her cheeks. She shivers in ecstasy.

Another night: the baby monitors hum tonelessly. The Daddy stares at his unshaven face in the mirror. Three mornings and three nights the Mommy has been away. The panic begins to creep in, the leading edge of the storm. He sits on the ground, tries to stretch out his legs, but a terrible pressure grips his chest. He cannot think. He stumbles to the bath, fills it with hot water, immerses himself. The loneliness swallows him up.

When the Mommy steps through the door, the world begins anew. She embraces the girl first, then the boy. Her back is stiff from the overnight flight. The Daddy feels like falling to the ground. Her singsong voice fills the house. His heart is overfull. He is a simple creature.

Another morning: the wind has broken. The first dry chill of winter electrifies the air. The girl delights at the sight of her breath. The Mommy moves to her own joyful tempo as she loads the children into the car. The Daddy carries his board to the beach. In the cold, rolling water, he leaves his body, communes with dolphins, reaches out to the spirits and energies that light up the world.

Later, his truck pulls up to the school. The girl's eyes shine when she sees the surfboard and the Daddy's hair still wet. She climbs into the car seat. Her tender, chilly fingers touch the Daddy on his bare shoulder, and all his doubts vanish . . . torn apart like wisps of cloud.

Inlets of the Mind

~~~~~~~~~~~~~~~~

This profile of the artist Bruce Reynolds originally ran in *The Surfer's Journal,* along with full-color pictures of Bruce's artwork, a photo of the artist and Kelly Slater in Bruce's workshop, and a shot of Bruce surfing overhead Cloudbreak, in Fiji. Kelly and Bruce's dynamic conjures Johnny Depp and Keith Richards, truth searchers, sometime conspiracists, discoursing on shadow governments or cetacean telepathy. At the café, over açai bowls, their flow is interrupted every half hour or so when Slater is obliged to rise from his seat and indulge another selfie seeker. When I asked Kelly if he wanted to write an intro to this article, he readily agreed. In true writerly fashion, he waited until the final day of deadline and penned four hundred words. Here they are:

Hometown Groundings

Bruce calls me Mr. Literal. It stems from the fact that I (we) enjoy dissecting the origins of everyday euphemisms while expounding on the literal nature of their meanings. We sort of become different characters around each other as a release from our regular lives. We work on our golf swings, talk politics, and chase alligators on the golf course. We theorize a better world and figure out ways to say what we think and feel through our mediums.

I live a busy life traveling the globe, meeting interesting people, experiencing endless cultural differences, attempting to comprehend and take in as much of this life as possible after having grown up with big dreams in a small town. When I'm home in that small town of Cocoa Beach, most afternoons are spent with Bruce. Although he lived on the West Coast for a period of time, he's spent the bulk of his life in this place, enamored with the simple pleasures a predictable small

town affords a person. He's got his restaurant he runs with his won-
derful wife and a regular clientele, most of whom he's on a first-name
basis with. His son has dived deeply into Brazilian jiujitsu and quickly
gone from a shy kid without a real direction to an unassuming assas-
sin in a few short years. You'd never know Bruce was his father while
watching his aggressive offensive attack. It's quite literally the opposite of Bruce's good nature and willingness to give anyone the stage
before himself. Bruce's martial art is displayed through his mixed-
medium art pieces, provocative and heartfelt, wittingly expressing a
more worldly experience and view than one might think a quiet family man might have living in this place.

Bruce tells me he lives vicariously through my travels and feels like
he soaks up the experiences I encounter. He, in turn, grounds me
back in my roots. We've got a good thing, me and Bruce. His art pieces
are an ode to a bigger picture, one that defies small-town politics and
mindset, subliminal messaging that's hidden yet somehow glaringly
obvious. It's said that art is the expression of one's soul. Bruce's art
probably looks a bit quirky, like his personality, but the deeper meaning keeps people wondering if they really know all of Bruce and what
stirs in that mind of his.

—Kelly Slater

Walking into Café Surfinista in Cocoa Beach, Florida, feels like sliding
into the brain of a slightly tripped-out Reno Abellira, circa 1971. A pas-
tiche of cork, porcelain, sea glass, brick, and pecky cypress lays back-
drop to expressionist paintings, classic surfboards, midcentury-modern
couches, and vintage posters for *Rainbow Bridge* and *Morning of the
Earth*. An old Honda café racer leans to one side, seemingly just off a
Mojave crossing. *The Sunshine Sea* plays on a cluster of five TV sets—five
Keith Paulls surfing five perfect blue rights somewhere in the Bay of Bis-
cay. Behind an elevated stage, an oracular vision of Duke Kahanamoku,
in his white-lion phase, stares at you from behind giant sunglasses, like
God or Dr. TJ Eckleburg.

If you arrive early enough, you'll find Bruce Reynolds relaxing into
a coffee at his regular high-top. The artist is trim, sunbaked, and well-
salted, with muscled forearms and the rough-sanded paws of a tree
carver or a lifelong surfboard shaper. He's as local as they get here in
Cocoa Beach.

Reynolds takes slow sips. His motions are drawn out and casual, contradictory behavior when you consider the manic, nerve-splitting intensity of his artwork.

Take the portrait on the wall behind him: a warped ink rendering of the country singer Johnny Cash—distended, with one eye bulging off his face. Pencil hatchings, conceivably added by a mischievous child, are scribbled all over the canvas. A three-wave set rolls and pitches beneath a Dewey Weber–style logo for "Surfboards by Johnny Cash." Up in one corner, the words "Folsom Prison Glassing Co." are scrawled in chalk on a section of blackboard. The piece vibrates, shimmers with madness. What's the message? Perhaps this idiom, scratched in all caps near the singer's mouth, offers a clue: "I WALK THE NOSE."

Pop-culture references, lines from well-known songs, Fibonacci spirals, defiant riddles: these are the ingredients in the Bruce Reynolds oeuvre. His work is nearly impossible to classify since the medium is ever-shifting. Now a folk painter, now a collagist, now a found-object sculptor. Even this café—a collaborative vision with his wife, Diane—is an immersive art experience, an architectural study in lyrical abstraction.

"Someone came in yesterday wanting to buy that Johnny Cash," Reynolds says with a chuckle. "I didn't know what to tell him."

Reynolds doesn't do self-promotion. His view is that the acts of creating and selling are antithetical to each other. Though his work has been exhibited in galleries and museums from Durban to Los Angeles, most of his art ends up, almost by accident, in the homes of private collectors. Surfers, in particular, are attracted to his pieces. John John Florence and Kelly Slater both own Reynolds originals.

His art studio connects to the leeward side of the café and lays out like a hangar for light aircraft or seaplanes: soaring, corrugated ceilings, a faint sargassum smell wafting in on the sea breeze. The space is cluttered with old bicycles, lifeguard signs, mannequin torsos, rusted tools, Cadillac hubcaps, tubes of paint, lantern bulbs, voodoo dolls of Mick Fanning. It's like a Terry Gilliam or Jeunet and Caro movie. Everything is degraded, filthy, reckless . . . and yet a meticulous sense of design and placement belies the chaos.

If it's true, as some suggest, that a person's psyche crystallizes in their thirteenth year, then Reynolds is an authentic product of 1968. Year of 'Nam, Nixon, and Nat Young, a country in upheaval, a spiritual flood.

It was the year all the kids grew out their hair, sawed down their long-boards, got *involved*.

Coming up at the Canaveral Pier, Reynolds watched local surfers like Dick Catri, Claude Codgen, Mike Tabeling, and Gary Propper go off and win major contests in Hawaii and California. "Surfing was everything," Reynolds says. "It was every waking moment, every part of you. It was a real, true subculture. And it was secretive, parts of it. You were doing something so great that the rest of the world had no clue about."

The waves are fickle in Florida, and for every one day the offshores, tide, and swell coalesce into groomed warm-water lines, there are one hundred days of side-chop, mush, shorepound, and wind-slop. An insatiable feast-or-famine mentality germinates in the soul of the Florida surfer at a very young age.

In 1974, inspired by the travel articles of Naughton and Peterson, Reynolds and three friends loaded their boards into an old green Econoline van and drove through Texas into Mexico and the Sierra Madre. They posted up near Mazatlán, where they made camp and rode hard until their money ran out. Instead of heading back to Cocoa Beach, they bolted up the West Coast, and the Econoline ended up in San Clemente. "There are periods in your life where all you do is surf," Reynolds remembers. "Some times were higher pitched than others."

For the next ten years, he sought the pure line, surfing the most consistent breaks on the mainland—Trestles, San Onofre, Salt Creek. When Cocoa Beach shaper Rich Munson returned from a stint on Kauai, spinning tales of the mysto breaks west of Hanalei Bay, Reynolds packed up a couple of boards and hitched a flight across the Pacific. He set up a tent at Ha'ena State Park and, captivated by the rights breaking over the outer reef, took the long paddle out to Tunnels by himself.

"Surfing the raw, big, exposed waves of Hawaii that season changed the direction of my surfing," Reynolds explains. "For me, it wasn't real radical. It was always trying to be as smooth and as long as possible."

In the mid-'80s, looking to lay down some roots, Reynolds returned to Cocoa Beach, where he took to salvaging discarded furniture from the side of the road and cobbling the fragments together into high-end studio tables and architectural cabinets. He'd gleaned some woodworking and trim carpentry skills in California, and by blending woods and metals with rivets, beads, and burned-in accents, he fashioned curios that sold well on the craft furniture circuit.

His experiments soon became more absurd, his colors starker, his boxes more free-form and visceral. Recurring images—the Vitruvian Man, Einstein, Elvis, the Bronzed Aussies—would pop up inside these early constructions. Reynolds's artistic technique was untrained, naïve, outsider. But the composition was intuitive and effective, and his pieces were commissioned by Laguna Beach art galleries, architectural firms, museums in Florida, and Disney's Festival of the Masters.

Many artists would have continued mining this vein, but Reynolds, loath to repeat himself, abandoned the 3D structures altogether and pivoted to a new form of expression: photomontage. "I think Oscar Wilde put it best," he says. "'Consistency is the last refuge of the unimaginative.'"

There is a theatrical sensibility to his collages—the players lined up on the stage, projecting their voices to the back of the house. Photos of characters culled from old *Life* magazines or children's picture books are adorned with dunce's caps, eye patches, or crosses, affixed to Lucky Strike boxes, and placed on the vertical sections of breaking waves. Whimsical or subversive text—the protean slips of the surfer's subconscious—sometimes accompany them: "Let my people surf." "No wankers." "Locals only." Fastidiously crafted, replete with hidden detail, the best of these evoke the sardonic, nonsensical works of Dada artists like Robert Rauschenberg, Raoul Hausmann, and Hannah Höch.

Next came a series of neo-expressionist paintings introducing the "Surfinistas," a gang of mythic revolutionaries whose sole purpose in life was, according to Reynolds, "to take the drop, set the edge, and let the rail run." Fauvist-styled skulls, off-kilter eyes, bared teeth, and rippling sea-blue skin channeled the strung-out energy of true surf addicts, either jonesing for a wave or in the euphoric thrall of the first ride of a dawn patrol. This phase coincided with the 2007 opening of Café Surfinista, an oasis for core Cocoa Beach locals and a much-needed counterweight to the plastic kitsch and commercialized kook culture of Ron Jon and the tourist traps to the north.

Cocoa Beach is an insular community, and it was only a matter of time before Slater strolled into the café and struck up a conversation with Reynolds. The two had played tennis together during the surf prodigy's high school years, and they rekindled their intergenerational friendship. "We've got a similar sense of humor," Reynolds says. "Kelly has an analytical mind, and we're both fascinated by innovation."

Slater became an admirer of Reynolds's artwork, and in 2015, when the presidential primary races turned into a shark feeding frenzy, he suggested the artist document the contentious election cycle with a show. Reynolds agreed and turned to the medium of assemblage. All the junk he'd hoarded over the years—from redneck flea markets, garage sales, plucked off the roadside—came together to form *Apolitical Process,* a poignant burlesque of the circus freakshow of Republican and Democratic candidates.

"Found-object stuff, it reminds me of stonework," Reynolds says. "The best flagstone masons never put down a piece once they pick it up. They invite the right stone into their hand. There's a serendipity to it." One notion that springs from this method is that the work cannot fail to astonish because the artist himself is consistently being surprised.

The centerpiece of that show, *The Great Wall of Trump,* invokes a trinity of personality cults: Adolf Hitler in boxing gloves, Donald Trump in shepherd's robes, and Chairman Mao with the body of a cow. The trio spars and poses over color fields of red, white, and blue. A naked woman, her eyes blacked out, sits atop the rod of Trump's frayed American flag. Below these strongmen, in a miasma of oppressive darkness, are disembodied baby doll heads, Black muscle figurines, blades, mousetraps, wires, and the Mexican flag slung through with coil nails. Looking at *The Great Wall of Trump* now, years later, you get the feeling that the line between farce and tragedy has grown finer and more tenuous than ever before.

A good number of the assemblages took aim at Trump, but Reynolds didn't spare the opposing side. In *Another Quality Job,* he painted Bill and Hillary Clinton in the deranged mode of the Surfinistas, a nightmarish portrait boxed in by nude Barbie dolls sealed in amber. A miniature VW bus called *Free Ride*—built out of bowls, bamboo sticks, cabinet knobs, and multicolored fabrics; up on blocks, it looked like a Marcel Duchamp ready-made—lampooned the socialist mores of Bernie Sanders.

PM Tenore, founder of RVCA and curator of Reynolds's exhibit, which opened in Venice Beach and was later displayed at the company headquarters in Costa Mesa, says, "I find myself getting lost in his multilayered sculptures as I explore all the nooks and crannies, always discovering a new element which augments the overall message of the work. Bruce's art amuses, holds your attention, and can change your perspective on the state of the culture, if not the world."

Duchamp once said, "Works of art are intermediaries in a process that the artist begins and the viewer completes." Just so, all of Reynolds's creations are up for interpretation. Perhaps the most stunning ones from the Venice show were his facsimiles of AR-15s—croquet posts, cameras, augers, rolling pins, and harmonicas intertwined and elegantly connected to form instruments of murder. Each faux gun was mounted on a sheet of whitewashed OSB. With the blood of the Pulse nightclub shooting still fresh in the viewer's mind, layers of meaning nested in the mock triggers and bullet chambers.

Bob Hurley, another surfer adherent to the Bruce Reynolds school, remarks, "What struck me most about Bruce's artwork was the satire. It was intellectual, political, and comical, but without being mean. There was that provocative thought in there that made you consider your own values."

For eight months, tinkering, hammering, and back drilling in the swelter of deep-red Florida, Reynolds summoned the energy needed to complete his ministerial gonzo show. But his investment in the news cycle left him feeling breathless, whacked-out, dizzy, as if he had taken a couple of set waves on the head. "That political stuff was real taxing," he explains. "I've since released myself from it."

After the election, Reynolds returned once again to his essence, forsaking the workaday life and traveling with Slater to surf transcendental sessions at Cloudbreak, Margaret River, Little Dume, Lemoore, and Haleiwa.

One effect of dedicating yourself to a life of continuous evolution is that your spirit will grow younger even as your body ages. Reynolds's central philosophy begins with a bottom turn. From there, it's all about simplicity, the natural line, the frictionless path. Set the rail and let the water do the work.

When the pandemic shut down the galleries and art shows, Reynolds found himself spending more hours in the solace of his home studio, a little backyard hut under the shade of a gumbo-limbo tree. There he painted a series of folk portraits of iconic personalities—Bruce Lee, Jimi Hendrix, Johnny Cash, Greg Noll—alongside proverbs and surf-themed double entendres. In a takeoff of *A Clockwork Orange*, the *Tavarua Milk Bar* serves as precursor to "a bit of the old ultra surfing." Another canvas has Clint Eastwood "going down to shoot the pier." In *Lost in Translation*, a jumbo samurai head is placed atop the body of David Byrne, who holds his surfboard out like a katana.

Some of Reynolds's most exquisite pieces have emerged from this latest period. The smaller collage/paintings present the spectator with beautiful puzzles. A tribal-patterned wave in *Moondance* seems to have

Bruce Reynolds, *Purple Waves*, 2021, acrylic, paper, and graphite on canvas.

Photograph courtesy of Bruce Reynolds.

landed there from the sky rather than from the artist's hand. In *Purple Waves,* a messianic Hendrix floats among words of diverse fonts: "And the Offshore Wind Cries, Mary." The waggish triptych *Celebrity Surf Check*—starring John and Yoko, Hunter S. Thompson, and David Bowie with boards tucked under their arms—approaches, in its balance, color, and simplicity, the culmination of neomodern humor painting.

"You're teaching yourself a new language," Reynolds says. "You keep speaking it. Not everybody understands. It's a different form of communication." Then, cracking a smile for the first time, the inner jester finally shows himself. "I always thought surfing was more avant-garde than it actually is."

There is a moment, as the artist sets his brush between his fingers, when the universe vibrates, his sense of time and self diminishes, and every movement is guided by a cosmic rhythm. Bruce Reynolds, the Surfinista, is still out there, still doing it, still learning. The secret, he realizes, is pinioned between thought and action, just as in that instant when the sea rises up from behind, when nothing else matters but the drop.

Core Surf

Cocoa Beach likes to advertise itself to visitors and would-be residents as "Mayberry-by-the-Sea"—a tropical, quaintly parochial town. The south side fits the bill well enough: Young parents push strollers past cafés, ice cream parlors, and shop fronts festooned with pink plumeria and hibiscus. Barefoot kids bicycle by with fishing rods. Everything is fragrant and freshly washed with rain, and all within walking distance—the public library, the skatepark, city hall, the Kelly Slater statue, the jazz club. At the hardware or grocery store, locals know each other by name and fall into easy, convivial conversations about gardening or turtle nesting season.

The north side, on the other hand, is a beach-kitsch tourist trap: snowbirds in floppy-brimmed hats stumble past tawdry T-shirt stores masquerading as surf shops. Plump, pasty families from Michigan and Ohio seem lost amid the traffic, motel signs, and chain restaurants. Looming over it all, in a ridiculous shade of dandelion yellow, is Ron Jon, that tacky surf-brand megalopolis, peddling its soft-tops, plastic tikis, and Chinese pop-out boards to day-trippers and theme-park run-off. Though Ron Jon still boasts a world-class surf team—notably Olympic gold medalist and world champion Caroline Marks—and provides a taste of authentic history in the Florida Surf Museum, for those who remember its charming origins on the pier, it feels like a palimpsest of another age, the ruined temple wall in the heart of East Coast surfing's Jerusalem.

Continue north toward the Cape and you'll find a true vestige of yesteryear: Core Surf, one of the few soulful old-school shops. Dennis Griffin, the proprietor, will meet you there with wet, rumpled hair and Buddhist nonchalance and guide you through his art-house collection of vintage East Coast boards. A Gary Propper Noserider from 1966; a wide-body thruster shaped by Jim "The Genius" Phillips; an early Mike Tabeling fish in ultramarine blue; an exquisite Pat O'Hare longboard with perfect pin lines and xanthic tint; a beat-up old Oceanside log from 1963. Hanging from the ceiling are classic Quiet Flight, Natural Art, Ocean Avenue, and Spectrum boards. If you're lucky, a masterpiece might twinkle at you from the used-board rack, a hand-shape from one of the local magicians: Larry Mayo, Chris Birch, Ricky Carroll.

Lanky kids lurk in the back of the shop, palming the rails, mind-carving. Kids of the post-Sebastian, ride-anything generation. Kids who avenged their grandfathers' murder of the longboard by resurrecting it, who learned to play contrapuntal harmonies. Long, short. Midlengths, fun shapes, eggs. I've seen them out in the water, Core Surf kids, charging hurricane swells on leashless shortboards at Driftwood House, and I've seen them on pigs, hanging ten on 8-inch waves at the Jetty.

"Living here, where windswell is what you get on offer, the more variety of crafts you have, the more days you'll get in the water, the more fun you'll have," Griffin tells me. By his own estimation, Griffin surfs more than three hundred days a year. There is something childlike to his commitment to surfing in the face of any and all conditions, and doing it well. He scouts the sandbars, finds the choicest option, pulls out one of the old boards from the '60s or '70s, and channels the surfers of the past.

One little-known truth about Brevard County is that on any given afternoon, the sandbars will undergo a surprising transformation, and two-block-long A-frames will materialize out of a deep-green nothingness. These sneaker swells—locals-only events—never last long; the wind goes dead, and for those brief Orphic hours, everything becomes so silent that the music of your rail slicing the silken hills sounds just like the tearing of fabric.

And here is the secret to how a surfer can get so good in Cocoa Beach. When it happens, it really happens. Take as many waves as you like. By the time the mainlanders cross the bridge, you'll have ridden fifty clean waves, and the wind will already be clocking from the east.

The kids understand. Kids like Gavin Idone, rope thin, raven-haired, seventeen, a noserider out of Cape Canaveral who might be confused for a young Tabeling in the backlit dawn. Or Indialantic's Saxon Wilson, styling into the ranks of the Duct Tape on '60s single-fins and Core Surf theology.

I was never a child of Cocoa Beach, so maybe I'll perceive it always through a filter, a gauzy veil that hangs over all those golden yesterdays.

But I've raised my children here and taught them to read the clues. It is natural to them that the ocean is waiting at the end of every street, that the sun will both rise and set over the water, and that on various moonless evenings, under a sky just bright enough to surf by, they might encounter Claude Codgen—half man, half unicorn—cruising the gloaming on his 9'6" Sunshine Surfboards noserider, his fingers projecting light.

Noseride Obsessive

Every time I hear the 1962 bossa nova song "Desafinado," my mind summons a vision of a willowy, teenaged Joel Tudor noseriding at Ehukai Beach Park. The sea is a washed-out jade green, the afternoon sun has transmuted his skin to brushed gold, and he's riding in 3/4 time, winging his red Takayama to the improvisations of Stan Getz on tenor sax. It's impossible for me to avoid this musical association, this sonic madeleine. The image is burned forever into my brain as a result of frequent, obsessive rewatchings of the opening sequence of the surf film *Longer* at a time in my life when noseriding meant nearly everything to me.

If I'm being honest, noseriding still means nearly everything to me—it's that rarest of life's pleasures, the "nowhere you'd rather be" moment, the hallucinatory flow-state, the prolonged culmination, something on the level of the barrel ride or the tantric climax—but it was during my learning phase, when I was taking my nascent cross steps and feeling those first breaths of wind under my toes, that *Longer* took up permanent residence in my DVD player.

I still watch it, more than twenty years later, and still consider it to be the finest noseriding movie ever made. The fact that much of the thirty-nine minutes of footage features Tudor on twin-fins, fishes, and mid-lengths (the aphorism on the DVD cover reads: "open your mind and your boards will follow") only intensifies those dazzling scenes in which he is working the front rail.

The film's director—a Delphian figure known only as JBrother—possesses a brilliant, sommelieric ability to match his subject to his soundtrack. In his 1995 film *Adrift,* he opens audaciously on a thigh-high crumbler of a wave, with a child-like Tudor tango-stepping to the Beastie Boys' "Son of Neckbone." Other pairings include Donald Takayama noseriding backside to "E Mama Ea" and Nat Young carving to Mozart's *The Magic Flute* overture. In *Adrift*'s final scene, Tudor drops calmly into double-overhead Pipe on a nine-four longboard (with no leash) and swings under cover to Nina Simone's gospel version of Bob Dylan's "I Shall Be Released."

Longer debuted in 2001, the same year as *Momentum: Under the Influence,* and served as a sort of soft-power foil to the Taylor-Steele punk/shralp shortboard pictures of the post–New School generation. If the Andy Irons audience didn't quite have the patience for small-wave logging set to jazz, a niche group of noseride-obsessives (myself among them) did—and we sat back in marijuana-tinged bliss, reveling in the subtle play around the melody, the recursive tacks and adaptations, the slack carelessness, and the timeless affinities between jazz and stylish longboarding.

"Desafinado" rolls into its final verse, and Tudor arches into another wave, rising in slow motion like a cobra. In two steps he's on the nose, trimming, deep in the all-knowing pocket, guiding himself through space-time via microscopic shifts of body weight and gentle flexings of the ankles. His board is a whisper in the wave behind him, then it is gone completely, and only the man remains, flowing through every rimple. Charlie Byrd plucks his guitar; the double bass thumps in time. The high-speed sizzle, the impressionist gleam—the whole thing feels like a cool, sophisticated LSD trip.

Pause the film anywhere and you'll understand why trying to describe the physics behind this kind of noseriding requires a dose of magical thinking. It's like explaining how Kobe Bryant could levitate a few inches over his defender even after he was already on his way down. It's a clear flouting of science, a force propelled by absurdist principles or divine mysteries.[1]

What makes Tudor's ride at the Ehukai sandbar even more extraordinary is his positioning on the face of the wave. The lip line is chipping at the height of his shoulder. Compare this to photographs of noseriders

1 In *The Physics of Noseriding* (2022), Lauren Hill employs stunning deck-mounted camera shots to illustrate the hydrodynamics of the Coanda Effect, wherein water displaced by the front of the surfboard enfolds the tail "like a blanket" to lock the vessel in place. Suction is only one of the innumerable variables in play on a noseride. As water strikes the legs (especially backside, where it can't sluice free over the insteps), it creates drag. One must also consider the fin, providing submerged tension and keeping the tail from slipping out of the wave. The weight of the rider and construction materials of the surfboard dictate buoyancy and fluid thrust, not to mention the multiform differential equations associated with rail contours, nose template, hips, foil, thickness flow, rocker, etcetera.

at your local break. You'll almost never see the wave above the surfer's waist. Riding at such a precarious elevation requires—more than just superhuman rail instincts and bravado—a willing suspension of disbelief.

The best noseriders have a preternatural ability to see the future, to presage the critical section and plan accordingly. Should you fade into the peak or race immediately at an angle down the line? Body English plays a role, too—lean to the inside rail and elevator up the face, or tilt to the outside and drop your altitude? There's also this: in order to get to the nose in the first place, you must traverse the length of the deck. This sounds easy enough (walking, after all, is the most natural human motion), but the trick is to avoid looking like a rhesus monkey as you're doing it. Amateur noseriders will shuffle, get tangled up in their leashes, duck-walk, stink-bug, crab-claw, or run like fools ahead of the sweet spot, only to pearl on the shoulder. Cross-stepping to the tip, and remaining peaceful about it, requires a Taoist soul-mastery. Nowhere is this better exemplified than in *Longer*'s title sequence and Tudor's unbroken twenty-seven-second hang-five to "Desafinado."

The act of noseriding is at once a religious experience, a satisfaction of a desire, and an embrace of the impossible. It's not surprising that it rose to prominence in the late '50s and early '60s.[2] Like the jazz practitioners of that era, surfers extemporized, deviated from tradition, and reimagined freedom of movement. The spontaneous lines Miki Dora and Lance Carson were taking at Malibu shared wavelengths with what Coltrane and Parker were doing at the Village Vanguard.

When disco and cocaine came to snuff out the innocence of the '60s, jazz and noseriding went into hibernation, and all the adepts turned their focus toward radical turns, barrel rides, and eventually aerial maneuvers. Shortboarding offered a lighter essence, and the surface dance supplanted, for a time, the more elemental connection with the depths. A brief moment in the '90s saw performance longboarding flirt with the mainstream, but it wasn't until the turn of the century that art-house productions like *Adrift* and Thomas Campbell's *The Seedling* (1999) fully

---

2   Chances are noseriding's true provenance came centuries ago, with the ancient Hawaiians. Rabbit Kekai was perching as far back as the '40s, and doing it without a skeg, on a redwood hot curl. Dale Velzy and Mickey Muñoz were pulling toes over in California in the early '50s. But noseriding didn't peak until the '60s, when surfers like Nuuhiwa, Dora, and Joey Cabell took the art form to new dimensions.

resurrected the noseride. Working in the mode of *Rainbow Bridge, Morning of the Earth,* and George Greenough's *Innermost Limits of Pure Fun,* these films recalled the tenor and aesthetics of the '60s and set the stage for the neoclassical noseriding renaissance. By the early 2000s, a new generation of retro purists had arisen, and Joel Tudor emerged as their oracle.

Perhaps no better proof exists that the Aquarian Age is truly upon us than the ascendance of women as today's top world-class noseriders. Everything that makes longboarding appealing—the graceful gesture, the lack of contrivance, the casual glissade, the forward movement executed without aggression or hostility—finds its ideal expression in women. From a spectator's perspective, the sight of Kassia Meador, Kelia Moniz, Karina Rozunko, or Honolua Blomfield performing mudras in the high curl has certain advantages over watching Wingnut and Bonga Perkins smacking nine-foot logs against shortboard waves.[3] The males might have more raw power, but the females ultimately have more style.

Lauren Hill, the writer and director of *The Physics of Noseriding,* elucidates with this proverb: "Men tend to lead with their knees, but women, we go hip first." Which calls to mind two iconic images: One, David Nuuhiwa, that Apollo of noseriders, his body curved like a longbow, knees thrust forward, flying across a Huntington Beach wall. And two: Rell Sunn (in what might be the greatest noseriding photo of all time) hanging ten in her blue trunks, one eyebrow arched, hips far out ahead—a transcendentally chill sorceress.

This fearlessness, this inner harmony in the midst of a screaming noseride, is what separates the maestros from the mortals. To be utterly comfortable, down to your hands and fingers, especially in the face of an imminent upending, is possibly the end goal of all longboarders.

As for moving pictures, *Longer* maintains its place for me at the summit of the genre. It is simply the best noseriding footage ever stitched to song. I need only pull up the film's "Misty" sequence to find enough inspiration to paddle out into thigh-high closeouts on any given morning.

---

3   Part of the reason Tudor got hassled when he first came to the Islands as a youth was his long blonde hair, skinny frame, and balletic mien. The derisive nickname "Tinkerbell" carried certain misogynist implications. Years later, Tudor's contest series, the Duct Tape Invitational, displays significantly less chest-thumping combativeness and one-upmanship than the stuff seen regularly on the WSL. In fact, winning almost seems incidental. And Tudor was the first contest organizer to offer women the same prize money as the men.

The scene opens with a monochrome dissolve . . . semi-tragic conditions, 1–2-foot fizzling wind slop, a day that would have most surfers moaning and flailing. Tudor gathers speed easily, pivots low in the trough, and steps up the scales to the liquid trill of Erroll Garner's piano. Suddenly, he is slicing across the top of the wave, harnessing some previously hidden power. Everything is suggestion, like a Japanese ink painting, the wave a horizontal field of gray, Tudor himself a winged silhouette, like a pelican soaring on an updraft. With each turn, fronds of spray rise up from his tail. (The board is the Blue Messiah, a precursor to the Model T, so heavy, so deep-riding, that it manufactures its own sections.) The musical notes seem to sparkle on the water.

There is one stuttering instant when Tudor loses his balance and nearly plunges head-first into the soup. JBrother manages to syncopate this glitch with a pause, an empty space in the song. Here, we are made to understand how time can actually slow down for the greatest dancers and athletes. Just as a tennis ball swells to the size of a balloon for Novak Djokovic, or the basket is as large as a hula hoop when Steph Curry heaves a three-pointer, the wave cooperates with Joel Tudor, opening up possibilities unavailable to the faithless.

With a simple bow at the waist, he makes an epicritical adjustment, side-slips the tumbling rapids, and a new section appears, as if conjured there by the Blue Messiah. And there it is. Nothing could be simpler or more obvious than another run to the nose. No hesitation, no resistance. Just carry.

"It's a clear flouting of science, a force propelled by absurdist principles or divine mysteries." The author's wife, Brittany, perched on the nose.

Photograph by Louis Barr.

Openings

~~~~~~~~~~

On February 5, 2022, the world's most recognizable wave—the Banzai Pipeline—was sucking in long, liquid breaths and exhaling 10-foot sapphire cylinders over the shallow reef, and the world's most recognizable surfer—Robert Kelly Slater of Cocoa Beach—was paddling, tranquilly, in that precarious zone between the rise and the rumble, eyeing an incoming set with a mind toward Backdoor.

Pipeline is best known for its hollow, funneling lefts, but on certain north or northwest swells, an unconventional right forms off the peak, a sketchy, hit-or-miss, double-overhead, gut-check of a barrel ride known as Backdoor. Slater had been surfing Backdoor out of his mind during the opening rounds of the Billabong Pipe Pro (the prestige kickoff event of the World Surf League), and winning heat after improbable heat in the juiciest, cleanest, most flawless conditions he or anyone else had ever seen at a Pipeline contest.

What made Slater's run through the field so unlikely was not just his current ranking (eighteenth in the world), or his recent "career-ending" injury (he'd shattered two metatarsals and the Lisfranc ligament in his right foot, his driving pivot foot, and missed almost a year on tour), but the basic fact that Slater was one week shy of his fiftieth birthday. *Fifty*—an age at which a man can no longer feign childhood, when it becomes illogical to assume the knees and back will juke like they used to. Sure, the stray fifty-something yogi might still mix it up at your local shortboard peak, but the vast majority have long ago reconciled themselves to the deterioration of the muscles and joints and transitioned to higher-volume surfboards, or else quit the sport out of frustration. Yet here was Slater, going toe to toe with the kids, and surfing his way into the round of 16, where he faced off against twenty-two-year-old Hawaiian hotshot Barron Mamiya.

The crowd on the beach sat shoulder-to-shoulder on the golden berm, whistling, cheering, hoping for miracles. Mamiya was surfing his home break, and he immediately notched two solid rides, a 6.50 (out of 10) on a 6-foot left, and then a deeper, more critical, 8-foot drainer, spouting out of the deep turquoise cavern with an 8.67. Mamiya's combined score of 15.17 had Slater "comboed," meaning Kelly would still need two high-scoring waves to advance. About halfway through the forty-minute heat, Slater finally locked into a proper wave, an archetypal 8-foot Pipeline tube-ride and spit-out—good enough for an 8.00. But the clock was not working in the old man's favor. As the competitors waited for another set, a lull flattened the sea and made it look like a summer Florida day. With only eight minutes left, another set finally rolled in. Slater dropped into a beauty, stalled, tried to outrun a closeout section, and got swallowed up.

Unlike athletes in other sports, a professional surfer cannot depend solely on his own performance to determine his fate. At least half of the glory relies upon the vagaries of the sea. For more than forty years, Slater had nurtured a kind of occult connection to the wind and waves. And yes, the forces of nature had—on too many occasions to be luck or coincidence—sent the best waves in his direction just when he needed them most. But it had been six years since he had won a tour event. John John Florence and Seth Moniz and all the rest of the pro kids smelled it (respectfully): the bloom coming off the rose. But none of them, as yet, had been able to ascend to the throne. It was *time,* only time, that would end Slater's reign.

Another interlude shut down the waves, and the announcer began the countdown that would mark the end of Slater's wild run, and possibly his competitive career: "ten, nine, eight . . ."

There is no rational explanation for what happened in those final seconds. The ocean had been tossing waves Slater and Mamiya's way for the past forty minutes, but nothing at all like this thick, flexing A-frame wave that charged in over the reef at the very end of the heat. And there was Slater, in his red jersey, optimally positioned for the drop, slicing down the face of the majestic left, arms like gull wings—his right gripping the outside rail, his left fully immersed in the upward-surging wall of water—his whole body focused into an aggressive, twisting, forward lunge, the "backside attack" made famous by Slater himself at Pipe more than thirty years ago: back leg delicately, gracefully steadying the tail, all his weight over his front knee, driving with the left shoulder . . . A thousand people were screaming—a frantic sound, an early-era Beatles concert hysteria—as Slater vanished into the pit and stalled there . . . slowing down on purpose, locking himself into the chaos, traveling at the same speed as the wave. When the bullhorn blasted, signaling the end of the heat, the GOAT blew out in a white mist.

A few minutes later, Stephanie Gilmore was holding a microphone up to Slater's still-dripping face and asking, "What is that emotion that you're feeling?" Slater was temporarily unable to produce words. He was swallowing hard. His ice-blue eyes were rimmed with red, perhaps from the saltwater, perhaps from something else. He embraced his longtime girlfriend, Kalani, closed his eyes, and employed what appeared to be an advanced breathing technique. The whole thing seemed too scripted, too storybook to be true. But you can't write the ocean wave into the story. The ocean wave had come on its own. Everyone on the beach had seen it.

"Wow, that was crazy," Slater said, releasing his breath. "I couldn't believe it." His voice sounded like a twelve-year-old's.

It is rare for an elite athlete to compete at a sport's highest level anywhere past the age of forty. After Michael Jordan had lost some spring and explosiveness, he used his unparalleled court sense, coordination, and competitiveness to continue playing longer than most NBA guards. But even Jordan was done by the age of forty. Tom Brady, the "ageless wonder" quarterback, won his last Superbowl at forty-three. George Foreman, the oldest heavyweight champion (by a long shot), was forty-five when he knocked out Michael Moorer. Nolan Ryan, that Major League fireballer and defier of Father Time, finally retired at a Methuselan forty-six. When Jack Nicklaus won the Masters, also at age forty-six, he was considered ancient, *even for a golfer.* But Slater's secret was this: what his body had lost in explosiveness and kinetic energy he was able to draw from the water itself.

After his win over Mamiya, Slater outsurfed Kanoa Igaroshi in the quarterfinals, contorting himself through daring open-air drops, feather-kissing his rail down blue-green walls, waiting for that precise moment to compress, to *stick,* to redirect the momentum of his landing into the ideal speed line. Slater's magic persisted through the semis. His shaved head glimmering, he dodged the ten-ton paw of the lip and pocketed himself, surreally, into wave after wave, beating out Brazilian Miguel Pupo. Age be damned—Slater was surfing with all the frothing abandon of a grommet.

By the time Slater and Seth Moniz (of the Moniz clan, Hawaiian surf royalty) paddled out for the championship heat, the hive was pulsating on the beach, the *mana* was thick, and another miracle seemed inevitable. There was Slater, floating in the sun-bent reflections, eyeing that Backdoor set.

And wouldn't you know it.

It looked like an insane decision at first. Slater dropped in *way* behind the peak, too far to go right. But right he went, taunting the surf gods, scorching a high angle across the face and speeding momentarily under "the chandelier,"[1] until the wave hit a boil and closed out in front of him. The crowd groaned and lurched back, collectively, as Slater fell into the vortex. Only a few stray believers kept leaning forward, imagining some unseen fingers tugging at the cerulean curtain, teasing the wave, holding it open just enough to sustain their faith. Could Slater still be in there? Was there any chance, any space inside?

The roar that went up from the beach when Kelly came shooting out of that wave could have been heard in Kapa'a. He tried a hack off the lip, lost his balance, and crashed out on his back. It didn't matter. The barrel had provided a moment of what Kant might have called "dynamical sublimity." The judges awarded Slater a 9.0.

Only when you surf like you have nothing to lose do you open yourself up to divine wonders. On this day, at this contest, Slater touched the infinite. No one doubted, not really, what was about to happen. Two minutes remained on the clock, the swell was building, and the waves were the biggest they'd been all week.

Gerry Lopez once said this about Pipeline: "You're always on the edge . . . always hanging by your fingertips." Make one wrong move, let go a little too late, and you reckon with the reef.[2] Suddenly, here was Slater, scratching into one crazy, final wave, shunting himself over one last ledge. His fins completely disengaged on the drop; his heels left his

---

1 The origin of the chandelier metaphor to describe the delicate, crystal over-hang of a breaking lip is unknown, but it likely sprung from the mind of a surf magazine writer or photographer, possibly in the late '60s or early '70s. It has since been repeated ad infinitum by surf journalists, caption writers, and contest announcers, and reminds me of a quote by the Argentine poet Lugones, who said that "every word is a dead metaphor." Jorge Luis Borges would later remark that Lugones's statement itself was a metaphor, and added, "I think we all feel the difference between dead and living metaphors."

2 Pipeline is also the world's most lethal wave, claiming a surfer's life every three or four years.

board, so that his toes barely brushed the deck. Not many surfers, even pros, have the presence or instincts to land a fins-out 10-foot air drop at Backdoor. Still fewer can look up at a 14-foot wall of hulking closeout— with nowhere to go, no escape—and recognize the slimmest opening, the nearly impossible hope of salvation in the heart of the spiraling maw.

Now, with a little pounce, Slater juts upward. The brocaded curtain of breakwater almost beheads him, it actually *clips* him on the shoulder, but he absorbs the shock and wriggles up into the whorl . . . it's a tight squeeze, but he's in. Only the front tip of his board is visible from shore, leaflike in its tilts and flutters.

It's a massive, rampaging wave, and the wailing and crying is feverish on the beach—orgasmic—as the sea-god's fingers lift the lip back for a half second and Kelly materializes in his red jersey: styling, straight up *styling*, Lopez-like, running a hand on the kraken's face (imagine the energy, the flux of negatively charged ions a surfer must feel in one of these macking Pipeline barrels), before he vanishes another two seconds behind the last taper. When he emerges, weak-kneed, overcome, he covers his eyes with his hands and falls back like a man saved at a Pentecostal prayer rally.

Kelly Slater won the Pipe Pro a record eighth time, with the highest-scoring wave of the contest—a 9.77. They hoisted him aloft, carried him up the beach. "I don't know what to say, man," he told the WSL interviewer. "I committed my life to this." He was no longer swallowing down the tears, just letting them pour out, full stream. "This is the best win of my life."

The week on the North Shore had been wild, emotional, historic. The women had competed at the sacred arena for only the second year and proven themselves worthy gladiators. Moana Jones Wong had been crowned queen. When Kelly stepped up to the podium to accept the winner's trophy (his fifty-sixth, and likely his last)[3], he was still breaking up. It would have been impossible, in that moment, to find a happier man on Earth.

~~~~~~~~

3   As of this writing, Slater is fifty-two years old, an expectant father, and has purportedly retired from professional surfing for the third and final time, although he will likely continue to receive wild-card entries into contests and cannot yet be counted out at any of them.

A week later, and 5,000 miles away, Kalani was leading a blindfolded Slater by the hand into the front foyer of their recently purchased house in Cocoa Beach (an Apollo-era ranch-style on the Banana River in need of an update, or a full renovation, with lime-green wallpaper and shag carpeting in the bedrooms). A crew of fifty or so Cocoa Beach locals stood silently in the living room, holding their breaths. Not a flip-flop stirred on the terrazzo. Among them were Kelly's mom, his brothers Sean and Skippy, their wives, some high school friends, a few notable surfers (Matt Kechele, CJ Hobgood), the Cocoa Beach fire captain (Laitham Kellum, an elite foil-boarder whose wife grew up in this same house and whose memories were sprinkled into the shag carpeting), and Brittany and me, who had tagged along with Bruce and Diane Reynolds.

"OK," Kalani said. "You can look." When Slater pulled off the blindfold, the voices went up like a Greek chorus: "Happy birthday!"

Slater seemed genuinely surprised, even a little embarrassed. The vibe was mellow, familial, and sweet, a small-town pride for a local boy done good. But these Cocoa Beachers were used to seeing Slater pull off tricks like this, to the point where winning Pipe at the age of fifty seemed just another "Kelly thing to do."

I hadn't watched the Billabong Pipe Pro[4] or seen Slater's astonishing ride until Bruce Reynolds showed it to me on his phone that afternoon, in front of Slater.

"That's ridiculous," was all I could say.

Slater knew that I was a general contractor, so he and Kalani took us around the house, and we discussed the structural elements, bearing walls, ductwork, possible locations for bedroom additions and double-sided fireplaces. "I want this to be a family house," Slater told me, "a place where all the kids can come hang out. For the next generation."[5]

---

4   I've never been able to appreciate pro shortboarding contests; from a viewer's standpoint, most of the time is spent watching the surfers' heads bobbing in the water. The waves are impressive enough, but the maneuvers seem too uniform, too contrived, and the scoring too subjective (at least for me) to be entertaining for any long stretches of time. I also have a tough time accepting the concept of surfing as a competitive sport, rather than an expressive art form or naturalistic Shinto-type endeavor.

5   Slater had talked to me before about the "next generation." A few months back, he said, "It's my goal and my dream to build a really great wave somewhere around Cocoa Beach. I think that's the only way to build that hard-core surf culture back up, and create that next generation of kids who could go on to do big

The lot could easily accommodate a half pipe in the front yard, and a fifty-year-old beech tree by the river looked muscular enough to harbor an elaborate, multitiered tree house.

It was a cool, windless, late-winter Cocoa Beach afternoon, and we stood over the coquina bank, the sunlight pooling red on the water and glittering in the distant mangroves. "Have you been out there?" Brittany asked Kalani. "The Thousand Islands?"

"No," Kalani said. "Is it nice?"

"So beautiful. You paddle through these mazes and tunnels that open up into little lagoons, and you can't see any trace of civilization. It's like you're in another world."

"We used to go out there all the time when we were kids," Slater said.

Just then, two dorsal fins cut the lacquer in front of us, oil-black, pushing vees in the molten water. The dolphins surfaced and lolled there, gazing up at us with those smiling, clairvoyant eyes. Everyone drew in a little breath.

〜〜〜〜〜〜

They speak to those who listen—the spirits of that long-gone, barrier island tribe—in reverberations, in barely perceptible chants. You can hear them in the whistle of the river dolphins at sunset, or in the shiver of the sea oats in the west wind . . . ancient, phantasmagorical incantations . . .

I hear them today, as Kirin and I are crossing the dunes at Ninth Street. It's Easter, a cloudless morning, a 72-degree Florida idyll, A-frames crackling over the midbar. Ten thousand voices sing in the surging foam, in the millions of tiny shells scouring the shallows.

I'm taking out my 9'9" Mayo Noserider (teal-tint, full gloss, double stringer, square tail, pinched rails, 10-inch CJ Nelson fin set all the way back), and Kirin has his 7'9" Mayo Egg (matte pink, 3.5 inches thick, a midsize board that serves as a sort of mini-log for a fourteen-year-old his size). I haven't stepped foot in the water all week; it's electrifying—

---

things in other places. I really think we could create the best surf park experience in the world." He was referencing his "wave pool" technology; in 2015, Slater created "the longest open barrel high performance human-made wave in the world" in Lemoore, California, a machine-generated freshwater marvel, the quintessential surfer's fantasy of a reproduceable "perfect" wave. It seems fitting that the world's premier artificial wave would be invented by a Florida surfer who'd grown up desperate and starved for surf.

the rush a desiccated flower must feel when it's dipped into cool, fresh water—a current firing up the legs, torso, arms, and fingers, a rapid, jolting activation of the nervous system that climaxes with a pleasant sting on the lips.

Kirin hurdles over the incoming line of whitewater and strokes for the outside. I watch him fight through the impact zone, one foot raised behind him like a boomkin. When we make the calms, he sits up on his board and points to the eastern horizon. "Look at that," he says, his chest heaving. "You can see the curve of the earth." Only on such a coast, where the land is so profoundly flat, is the effect so revelatory—this vision of the dome of the world.

Lines haul in from the deep like long triangular prisms being pulled gently just below the surface. They collect soft, green, internal light. A cloaked figure appears inside one of these waves: a dolphin, roving in the glass. Why do they always appear in such moments of grace?

Now the wave reaches the culmination of its thousand-mile journey; it purrs and foments over the sandbar. Kirin pivots his board. He takes the drop and is gone.

Is there anything better than being young, when all the world is still new, and all your senses keen and eager and finely attuned? From behind, I can see him cruising, backside, on a right, riding in that leisurely, naturalistic style possessed only by the lucky few who grew up on the water and learned to surf in infancy.

I take the next wave, a long, easy right—tall and cool and thirst-quenching as a glass of lemonade. On the inside, I pass Kirin as he's paddling back out through the soup. His face is lit up like one of Raphael's cherubs.

When we meet again, we've drifted a block north, to the Eighth Street church steeple. A coterie of twenty or so longboarders are scattered here, in a loose pack. One of them is Ben Malik, the former mayor of Cocoa Beach, and an old friend. "Good sandbar?" I ask him.

"Guess the secret's out," Ben deadpans.

Kirin and I float out into deeper water, content to keep our distance from the others. The Eighth Street sandbar has gained a reputation recently, through whisper networks and group chats, as "the only spot that's breaking." The sandbar is good here, though in truth it's not much better than at Eleventh or Thirteenth. But surfers are social creatures, and the breaks in Cocoa Beach are such uncertain propositions that locals will often choose to surf in a crowd rather than risk a wasted session at a troughed-out spot, of which there are many. Today, there are enough waves for everyone, and some of the classic old-timers are killing it. We watch as Mark Grabowski, a no-name local legend, carves a shoulder-high left on his midlength, gull-winging through floater after floater. A hundred yards beyond him, there's a wedding party on the beach; I can make out the bride in her white dress, a gaggle of pale northerners in beige three-piece suits and frilled lavender gowns. A groomsman marches down to the water's edge, flings off his jacket, and walks into the ocean. As a wave strikes his thighs, his hoots carry on the west wind. He stumbles into the trough, raises his arms, and spins round like a man dancing the hora. Two bridesmaids dash after him into the shallows, shrieking rapturously, their skirts aflutter in white lattice. It's an impromptu Easter baptism, a tourist absurdity, but it's touching, in a way, a reminder that to set foot in the sea is to engage in an act of faith.

Surf long enough and you develop a sixth sense for when the cleanup set[6] is imminent. There's a smell, or a lack of smell, a sort of vacancy in the air that precedes its approach. "Let's paddle out a bit," I suggest. We set up camp on the far outside. Off in the west, across the rippling blue quiltwork, I see two familiar sparks of color on the beach—a wondrous, heart-stabbing vision—Brittany and Aubrey, crossing the dunes with their surfboards, coming out to join us.

My instincts about the oncoming set are justified. Blue-leather hills mount in the east and darken the foreground. The first wave is head-high, overhead on Kirin, but there's a wobble to it. "It's closing out," I tell him. "But check out the one behind it." The next wave swings north, setting us up at the sloping edge of the wall, offering the proposition of a makeable left, an opportunity to outrun the peak. As the first wave passes under us, we rise up into the wind, then sink down again into the trough.

I give Kirin the nod. He turns and goes. I take off behind him.

To tap into the rhythm of the sea is to connect at a basic, pulsating level with what it means to be human. The lungs contract and expand. The heart thrums. So much about what is enjoyable about surfing is the lead-up, the anticipation, the effort in advance of the rapture. Like lovemaking, surfing is made all the sweeter for the waiting.

How can you lay down that sensation in words? A winged angel, slic-

---

6   Cleanup set: A group of outlier waves, markedly bigger than the prior sets, which can send surfers duck-diving or ditching their boards in a panic as it obliterates everyone in the lineup and washes it clean.

ing the sea? "One is caught up and hurled shoreward as by some Titan's hand." There's Jack London again. The Hawaiians called it *he'e nalu*—wave sliding. The Ais must have had their own name for it. Sadly, lost to time. Riding behind my son, borne along on that phase change, that transitional fringe between water and wind, I react, chemically, to the forces of drag, suction, and outflow, to the liquid energy that guides us all.

Probably it sounds too trivial, too fatuous, to compare the psyche of a surfer to that of a child chasing after bubbles. Then again, what could be more serious, or more sublime, than that euphoric quest? To a child, whole universes abide in those iridescent rainbows.

Here, on Florida's barrier island, you learn to be grateful. To keep the waves with you, even after they have broken and dissipated. To listen for the voices, gathering and straining through the vapor, reminding us that we are merely solid in flow state. Like the sand. Like the waves. Here and gone, we leave no mark.

ACKNOWLEDGMENTS

This book would not have been possible without the support of my Cocoa Beach friends: Matt Bellina (whose sage advice led me onto the true path), John Hughes at the Florida Surf Museum, Bob Freeman (one of the most classic surfers I know), Sean O'Hare, John Hearin, Phil Salick, Dennis Griffin at Core Surf, Jesse Restivo, Rick Piper, Bruce Reynolds, Tony and Athena Sasso, Ben Malik, the old Eleventh Street crew, the Vanns, Christmans, and Williamses, Laitham Kellum, Dave Miller (my first friend in Cocoa Beach), and all the hardcore rippers who I never got a chance to profile, including Sharon Wolfe Cranston, Mark Grabowski, Tom from 13th Street, Melody DeCarlo, and countless others. I'd like to thank all the surfers and shapers who were so generous with their time in support of this project: Kelly Slater, CJ Hobgood, Caroline Marks, Bruce Walker, Pete Dooley, Ricky Carroll, George Robinson, Jeff Crawford, Greg Loehr, Rich Munson, Ed Leasure, and especially Matt Kechele, who became a sort of guiding light for this book; the brilliant editor Sian Hunter, along with the whole publishing team at UPF; Brittany (my at-home editor and strict deadline enforcer); Mom, Dad, Jodi, Carly, uncle Gerry; Jonas Claesson for his gorgeous cover art; Ryan Rivas at Burrow Press, a true champion of Florida literature; Matt Warshaw (the oracle of surf history); Nick McGregor at *Eastern Surf*; everyone at the old *Surfer* magazine; and Scott Hulet, Alex Wilson, Whitman Bedwell, and Steve Pezman at *The Surfer's Journal*, without whom I would never have devoted so many hours to writing about surfing.

"How to Be a Kook" appeared originally in the *Beachside Resident*, as did earlier iterations of "Passages from the Surfer's Bible," "Why We Surf," "Slater, in Bronze," "A Field Guide to Spring Break, Cocoa Beach," "One Summer Day," and "Thoughts on the Cold-Water Season." "The Golden Age," "Youth Movement," and "Core Surf" were published first in *The Surfer's Journal* under the title "Space Coast." "Inlets of the Mind" and "Noseride Obsessive" also first ran in *The Surfer's Journal*. "Dick Catri, 1938–2017" appeared originally in *Surfer,* under the title "Honoring Florida's Original Surf Legend." The surfboard shaper profiles "Thickness Flow: The Larry Mayo Perspective" and "George Robinson: The True Line" were published in *Eastern Surf Magazine*. "Holding the Line" is a collection of material from a series of op-eds I wrote for *Florida Today* on Brevard County's sand-dredging projects. I am grateful to these publications for granting permission to reprint these essays.

A NOTE ON SOURCES

Information about the pre-contact Ais—the dominant Indigenous tribe on this barrier island for thousands of years—is somewhat scarce, despite the fact that their burial mounds and middens are scattered throughout the county. The definitive firsthand account of Ais culture remains *Jonathan Dickinson's Journal,* originally published in 1699 under the prolix (and suspect) title: *Gods protecting providence, man's surest help and defence in the times of the greatest difficulty and most imminent danger evidenced in the remarkable deliverance of divers persons from the devouring waves of the sea, amongst which they suffered shipwreck: and also from the more cruelly devouring jawes of the inhumane canibals of Florida / faithfully related by one of the persons concerned therein, Jonathan Dickenson.* Amy Turner Bushnell and Jason Daniels have edited and annotated a modern edition, *Jonathan Dickinson's Journal, or God's Protecting Providence: An Early American Castaway Narrative* (Florida Historical Society Press, 2023).

My descriptions of the Ais were also informed by the works of Dr. Peter John Ferdinando at UNC–Charlotte, especially his 2015 FIU dissertation, "Atlantic Ais in the Sixteenth and Seventeenth Centuries: Maritime Adaptation, Indigenous Wrecking, and Buccaneer Raids on Florida's Central East Coast." Dr. Fernandino was gracious enough to answer some questions I had about the Ais' stature and physical characteristics. Other Ais material that proved useful in my research came from *The Indians of the Southeastern United States* by John R. Swanton (Smithsonian, 1979), *Indians of Central and South Florida, 1513–1763* by John H. Hann (University Press of Florida, 2003), and the article "Summer Pentoaya: Locating a Prominent Ais Indian Town along the Indian River Lagoon, Florida," by Brevard County archaeologist Alan Brech (*Florida*

Anthropologist 60, no. 1 [March 2007]), with whom I had the honor of serving on the Brevard County Historical Commission.

I personally conducted all the interviews in this book, unless otherwise noted. The Dick Catri quotes came from his interview with Dennis Bennett in 2012.

INDEX

Page numbers in *italics* refer to illustrations or photographs.

Dan Reiter is a surfer, author, and a general contractor. He was born in Montreal in the time of Lévesque but moved to Florida at the age of three. His surf dispatches have been featured in *The Surfer's Journal*, *Surfer Magazine*, and *Eastern Surf Magazine*, and his short stories have appeared in *Kenyon Review*, *Tin House*, *Shenandoah*, *McSweeney's*, *Florida Review*, *Bellevue Literary Review*, *American Short Fiction*, and elsewhere. He lives in Cocoa Beach, Florida, on a dissolving barrier island.